THE POWER OF MEDITATION

Simple Practices for Mental Clarity and Relaxation

D1736628

JASON HEMLOCK

THE POWER OF MEDITATION:
Simple Practices for Mental Clarity and Relaxation
by Jason Hemlock

ISBN: 979-8375133539

CONTENTS

FOREWORD

A s a way of saying thank you for purchasing this book, I'm offering a four-page meditation tracker for free. You will also receive updates and future content from me when you sign up for my email list.

You can sign up here: bouchardpublishing.com/meditation

ALSO BY JASON HEMLOCK

Stoicism: How to Use Stoic Philosophy to Find Inner Peace and Happiness

Secrets of the Stoics: How to Live an Undefeatable Life

Practicing Stoicism: A Daily Journal with Meditation Practices, Self-Reflections and Ancient Wisdom from Marcus Aurelius

INTRODUCTION

---

*'The greatest thing in the world is to know
how to belong to oneself'*
—Michel de Montaigne

My meditation journey began back when I was a teenager. Born a few years too late to be part of the summer of love, I nevertheless fancied I had the soul of a hippie and was drawn to a counterculture that sang of flowers and sunshine, spoke of the dawning of a new age, and explored the limitless potential of the mind with various techniques – including meditation.

I explored a range of meditation practices, including breath work and mantra meditation. I used a mantra to chant myself to sleep and now my brain is programmed to use that same mantra every night when I feel sleepy. It's now over thirty years later and I can tell when I'm drifting off because my mind starts chanting, *I love you, I'm sorry, please forgive me, thank you...*

Now I meditate daily, and I have no doubt that it has had a positive impact on my life. On the rare occasions when I'm not able to meditate for whatever reason, I can feel myself becoming more agitated and quicker to anger. Meditation helps me connect with my natural inner state of calm and become less reactive to the world around me.

The word 'meditation' is derived from the Latin term *meditatum*, meaning 'to ponder.' Meditation allows us to explore our minds for a greater understanding of who we are and where we fit in the grand scheme of things.

To give you a little bit of insight into the history of meditation, it is frequently described as an ancient practice, but it is difficult to pinpoint exactly when meditation was discovered. There are some theories to suggest that meditation could well date back to the dawn of humanity, with possible evidence that Neanderthals were capable of meditating. Others believe that its origins lie in Eastern cultures and civilizations.

There are some old written Indian records dating back to around 1500 BC that mention the practice of *Dhyāna* or *Jhāna*, which involved training the mind, a practice that could be seen as meditation. Many of these records are from Hindu traditions, but there are even older mentions of similar concepts in Buddhist Indian texts, although these are considered more ambiguous when it comes to discussing meditation.

There are also references to meditative practice in ancient Chinese texts dating back to the 3rd and 6th centuries BC. There are many references to meditation techniques, such as *Shou Zhong* (guarding the middle), *Bao Yi* (embracing the one), *Shou Jing* ('guarding tranquillity'), and *Bao Pu* ('embracing simplicity'). Some scholars believe that it is virtually impossible to know whether these techniques were already in regular use at the time of writing or if they were invented specifically for the text. However, there are other references to meditative practices in early documents, such as the *Zhuangzi* (written sometime between 476–221 BC) and the *Neiye* from the 4th century BC.

The reality is that the precise origins of meditation are shrouded in mystery and probably always will be. However, while we do not know exactly how meditation was developed, there are some people who played an active part in developing and sharing the practice of meditation.

The Buddha (India)

The Buddha was a prince who turned his back on royal life to become a monk, philosopher, and religious leader. His teachings gave rise to Buddhism. While he didn't invent or discover meditation, Buddhist texts describe various meditative techniques and discuss how the Buddha studied with enlightened teachers to discover more about meditation and how it could lead to self-fulfilment. Although he might not be the creator of meditation, the Buddha played a significant role in raising awareness of the importance of it.

Lao-Tzu (China)

Lao-Tzu was a Chinese philosopher whose name is an honorific, meaning 'Old Teacher' or 'Old Master.' He is believed to be the author of the Tao-te-Ching, which details his beliefs and teachings that gave rise to the philosophical system of Taoism. Taoism incorporates many meditative practices, as well as the value and wisdom to be found in silence. Scholars are divided over whether Lao-Tzu was an individual or whether the title was given to a group of individuals and philosophers who followed the same principles. Regardless of whether it was one man or a collective, Lao-Tzu's work has had a major influence on the development of meditation.

Dosho (Japan)

Dosho was a 7th century Japanese monk who studied Buddhism in China under the guidance of the great master Hsuan Tsang. During his time journeying through China, Dosho learnt about Zen. He took the process back to Japan, where he opened a meditation hall devoted to the practice of Zazen, a type of sitting meditation. He built a community of monks and students all dedicated to teaching this form of meditation in Japan.

Meditation is referred to in many cultures and religions, including Judaism, Islam, Sufism, Jainism, Confucianism, and Christianity, and it has been practised across a broad geographical range and over the course of many centuries. As such, it transcends religion or race.

Meditation first started to gain popularity in the West during the 1700s. This was when some Eastern philosophical texts, such as the Upanishads, the Bhagavad Gita, and the Buddhist Sutras, were translated into different European languages and circulated.

However, in the 18th century, meditation was viewed as something to be confined to discussion and study by philosophers and intellectuals, such as Voltaire and Schopenhauer. It was only in the 20th century that meditation became more mainstream, particularly in the United States, after an influential yogi, Swami Vivekananda, gave a presentation to the Parliament of Religions in Chicago.

His talk generated new interest in the Eastern approach to spirituality among Western cultures. This rise in popularity inspired other spiritual teachers, such as Swami Rama (the Himalayan Institute), Paramahansa Yogananda (Self-Realization Fellowship) and Maharishi Mahesh Yogi (Transcendental Meditation), to take their philosophies and practices to the States. In addition, Buddhist teachers from movements, such as the Zen school of thought and Theravada school of thought, also journeyed to the States, where they found an eager audience.

As an individual practice, meditation has been influenced by the prevailing culture, adapting and changing to suit the needs of those who have grown up in that culture. As it became more established in the West, meditation became less steeped in religion, its principles being taught in more westernized ways.

By the 60s and 70s, meditation was being studied by scientists, which took it further away from being a solely spiritual practice and more toward something anyone could enjoy and benefit from, regardless of whether or not they were looking for spiritual fulfilment.

Herbert Benson was one of the first Western researchers to carry out studies on the effect of meditation on mental and physiological health in the late 1960s. In 1975, he wrote his best-selling book, *The Relaxation Response,* as well as founding the Mind Body Medical Institute.

During this period, Transcendental Meditation (TM) was increasingly popular, thanks to many celebrities studying it as a means to cope with the pressures of fame. The most famous students were the Beatles, who journeyed to India to learn from the Maharishi Mahesh Yogi, although John Lennon would later publicly discuss his issues with the Maharishi, leading him to turn his back on the practice of TM.

In the late 1970s, Jon Kabat-Zinn discovered meditation while he was studying at MIT. He began researching its health benefits and would go on to open his Stress Reduction Clinic in 1979, as well as launch his Mindfulness-Based-Stress-Reduction (MBSR) program.

In the 60s and 70s, meditation was still strongly associated with hippie culture, but in the 1990s, it started to become more mainstream.

In 1993, Deepak Chopra published his book *Ageless Body, Timeless Mind.* Following an appearance on *Oprah,* it sold over 137,000 copies in one day, taking meditation to the masses. More and more celebrities started to speak openly about the positive impact of meditation on their lives, which led to more books about meditation being published, further increasing awareness.

In the 1990s, mindfulness was also becoming more widespread. Williams, Teasdale, and Seagal built upon Kabat-Zinn's MBSR program to develop an approach to support those suffering from depression and anxiety. Mindfulness-Based Cognitive Therapy (MBCT) combined mindfulness with Cognitive Behavioural Therapy for an effective treatment. It was subsequently clinically approved by the National Institute for Clinical Excellence (NICE) in the UK and is now viewed as a treatment of choice for depression.

By 2012, there were more than 700 mindfulness-based programs being offered around the world. The MBSR program has been used in many studies on the effect of meditation. Now there is a wealth of resources and schools available for people to learn about meditation, and medical science continues to learn more about just how incredible meditation is in treating a broad spectrum of mental and physical problems.

I have personally experienced the benefits of meditation and it is my hope that this book will empower you to develop your own practice so you can see for yourself just how life-changing meditation can be. Through the course of this book, you will learn everything you need to know to get started with meditation, as well as discover a number of different techniques to explore to find the best approach for you. You'll find out how you know when you're actually meditating and what to expect – as well as the warning signs to know when meditation isn't right for you.

Meditation can improve and enhance your life in so many different ways. Read on, and discover the impact it can have on you.

CHAPTER ONE:

WHY ALL THE FUSS ABOUT MEDITATION?

*"The thing about meditation is you
become more and more you."*
—David Lynch

When I was part of a meditation group, our teacher gave us a group assignment to define meditation. You'd think it would be a simple task, but as we talked about it, it became increasingly apparent that it is very difficult to describe. It could be said that there are as many different definitions of meditation as there are meditators, which isn't exactly helpful when you're trying to find out what you're letting yourself in for!

One definition is that it is an inclusive, conscious relaxation technique. It is a structured awareness of yourself and the current moment, a training of the mind so you can experience yourself as you are without judgement at a time when you are totally in the moment, experiencing flow state as a natural way of being.

Meditation is *not* daydreaming or allowing the mind to wander. There is a structure or framework to it that keeps the mind focused. It is not the same for everyone - even if two people use the same technique at the same time, they will have different experiences. Likewise, when you use the same method repeatedly, you will have different results in different sessions.

It is not hypnosis or auto-suggestive, nor is it a way of relinquishing control of the self; you remain in charge of your experience and can choose to stop meditating at any moment. It is not suitable for everyone - there are some people for whom it is contraindicated, particularly with certain mental health conditions. Further, it is not prescriptive - it is about finding what works for you, not conforming to a list of rules.

There is a myth that you are supposed to empty your mind when you're meditating. I'm not quite sure how or why this myth arose because it is impossible to empty the mind or stop thoughts. Rather, meditation is about choosing what fills your mind.

However you choose to define meditation, it involves using a certain technique to engender a heightened state of awareness and focused attention to change your consciousness, which benefits the mind, body, and spirit. Some teachers liken consciousness to a stream that is constantly shifting and changes as it moves forward. Meditation is a method of changing the course of that stream, which subsequently changes how you perceive and react to the world around you. Everything is your perception, so when you shift how you view people and events, you can experience major changes in your mood and experience.

A brief history of the research into meditation

With the rise in popularity of meditation, it was only a matter of time before the scientific community started to study its effect. The very first piece of scientific research into meditation was in 1936, with the first study using an electroencephalogram (EEG) taking place in 1955. An EEG places electrodes across someone's head to measure the electrical waves of activity. This showed that there are verified changes in brain activity when someone meditates.

In the 1960s, Swami Rama, a senior Yogi from the Himalayan International Institute of Yoga Science, was the focus of research carried out at the Menninger Clinic in Kansas, United States of America. Gardner Murphy, an American psychologist, spearheaded the studies, which examined Swami Rama's abilities to control certain bodily functions that had been believed to be totally involuntary, like his heartbeat and blood pressure.

Across a number of studies, Swami Rama was able to show he could generate different types of brain waves on demand, including alpha, delta, theta, and gamma; alter his heartbeat, such as increasing it to 300 beats per minute for 16 seconds and stopping it completely for a few seconds; maintain awareness of his surrounding environment while his brain was in a deep sleep cycle; and change his skin and internal body temperatures.

Unsurprisingly, the results of these studies generated interest among the psychological and medical communities to look further into the physiological impact of meditation.

Herbert Benson and his colleagues, Greenwood, and Klemchuk, did research in the mid-1970s into the potential use of meditation to treat certain health issues. They found that meditation led to a range of physical and biochemical changes in the body, which Benson dubbed the 'Relaxation Response.' This discovery was ground-breaking, as until that moment, meditation had been believed to be a solely religious practice unsuitable for medical or health purposes. Benson's research was directly responsible for a shift in this thinking, which gave rise to further research into how meditation could be incorporated into healthcare.

Subsequent research examined the effect of meditation on the mind and body, particularly examining addiction, cardiovascular disease, and cognitive functioning. The findings were incredible, although in recent times, some of the results have been called into question, with peer-reviewed meta-analysis of the research determining that many results are inconclusive.

In 2000, the Dalai Lama met with a number of Western psychologists and neuroscientists to encourage them to study experienced meditation masters, using modern neuroimaging technology to examine the impact of meditation on the brain.

In 2007, the National Center for Complementary and Integrative Health published a review of 813 different studies into five different types of meditation: mantra meditation, mindfulness meditation, Tai Chi, Qigong, and yoga. They only looked at studies involving adults, and which investigated the effects of meditation on physiological conditions like cardiovascular disease, substance abuse, addiction, and hypertension. The researchers concluded that their review threw up a lack of quality methodology in studies focused on meditation, with no common theoretical perspective across scientific research. While they determined that there has been a clear improvement in how meditation had been studied since the 60s and 70s, they argued that there is still a long way to go if we are to truly understand how meditation works.

The benefits of meditation

Leaving aside the question of how exactly meditation works its magic, there is still an overwhelming amount of research that shows that meditation can have a positive impact on the mind and body. More studies are being performed all the time, adding to our understanding with the benefit of more rigorous methodology.

While results will vary from person to person, the benefits of meditation may include:

1. **Lower levels of stress**

   Needing to reduce stress levels is one of the most common reasons people turn to meditation. Many of those who use this technique report feeling less stressed after establishing a regular meditation practice.

   The reason for this may be down to the fact that meditation reduces both the physical and mental symptoms of stress. When we are stressed, the body produces more of the hormone cortisol, which is responsible for many of the negative effects of stress, such as the release of cytokines, or inflammatory chemicals. When your body is experiencing a stress response, you may suffer from difficulties sleeping, feel more depressed or anxious, and suffer from fatigue and foggy thinking. You may also find your blood pressure increases. One eight-week study showed that mindfulness meditation could reduce this inflammation response, lowering the physical impact of stress.

   Other research has also suggested that meditation could combat the symptoms of other stress-related conditions, such as irritable bowel syndrome, fibromyalgia, and post-traumatic stress disorder (PTSD).

2. **Lower anxiety levels**

   Given that meditation combats stress, it's unsurprising that it also reduces feelings of anxiety, which is closely linked to stress. One meta-analysis of almost 1,300 adults observed this correlation, with those feeling the most anxious reporting the greatest relief thanks to meditation. In addition, a study found that an eight-week program of mindfulness meditation could reduce anxiety symptoms in those suffering from generalized anxiety disorder, as well as improving self-talk and enhancing someone's ability to respond to and cope with stress.

Another study looked at people suffering with chronic pain and found that an eight-week meditation program had a discernible impact on their depression, anxiety, and pain in the months following the program.

Meanwhile, those struggling with anxiety because of the pressure of work can take heart from the study that found that where employees used a mindfulness meditation app for eight weeks, they felt better about themselves and their work compared to those who were in the control group (not meditating).

3. **Improves emotional wellbeing**
There is evidence to show that some types of meditation can improve your self-image and give you a more positive outlook on life. One review of a range of treatments given to over 3500 adults found that mindfulness meditation could improve the symptoms of depression. Another review looked at 18 studies and concluded that people who received meditation therapies had fewer symptoms of depression compared with those in the control group.

One study found that those who completed a meditation exercise had fewer negative thoughts when looking at negative images than those who were in the control.

4. **Gives you greater self-awareness**
Some types of meditation may help you learn more about yourself, supporting you to be your best self. For example,

self-inquiry meditation is specifically aimed at helping you understand yourself better and how you relate to the people around you.

Other types, such as mindfulness, support you to identify thoughts that could be harmful and self-defeating. As you develop a stronger awareness of the way you think, you can change these thoughts to be more positive and self-serving.

One review of 27 studies into tai chi demonstrated that those who practiced tai chi may experience enhanced self-efficacy (one's ability to believe in their capacity and ability to overcome obstacles). Another study followed 153 adults who used a mindfulness meditation app for two weeks. After this period, they claimed to be feeling less lonely and had increased their amount of social contact versus those in the control group.

5. Improves your attention span

Just like any muscle, you can improve the brain's function with practice. Focused-attention meditation can help to enhance the strength and endurance of your ability to focus on a task. A few studies have shown that those who meditated found it easier to pay attention and had more accuracy when completing a task compared to the non-meditators. One review even found that meditation could reverse habits of the mind that contributed to mind-wandering, worrying, and lowered attention span.

What's more, you don't have to meditate for long to experience these benefits. One study showed that just 13 minutes every day for eight weeks can improve an individual's attention and memory.

6. Reduces the impact of aging on memory

Contrary to the saying, you *can* teach an old dog new tricks. Because meditation can improve your attention span and clarity of thought, it may help keep your mind young.

Kirtan Kriya, or SaTaNaMa, is a type of meditation that brings together a mantra and a simple, repetitive movement of the fingers to focus your thoughts. Studies carried out with people suffering from age-related memory loss have shown that this particular type of meditation can improve performance on neuropsychological tasks.

One review discovered that there is evidence to suggest that a number of different meditation styles could improve attention, memory, and mental acuity in older study participants.

One exciting finding is that, in addition to combating natural age-related memory loss, meditation may help improve memory function in patients suffering from dementia. Not only that, it could also help those caring for those patients by reducing stress levels and enhancing their coping abilities.

7. Makes you kinder

Some forms of meditation have a lovely side effect – they increase your sense of compassion both towards yourself and others, making you feel and act with kindness. In particular, Metta, or loving kindness meditation, is focused on sending kind thoughts and feelings towards yourself and then to others. Many people struggle to love themselves, let alone allow anyone else to love them, and this type of meditation supports you to accept kindness and forgiveness for yourself before sending it out to others – loved ones, acquaintances, and even those we are having problems with or actively dislike.

One meta-analysis of 22 studies into Metta meditation concluded that it had a noticeable positive impact on people's compassion towards themselves and others. However, it's worth bearing in mind that one study of 100 adults who were randomly assigned to a program featuring loving kindness meditation found that the impact varied depending on much time people spent meditating. In other words, the more time someone spent on their Metta meditation practice, the better they felt. Another study that involved 50 college students found that doing a Metta meditation three times a week had a positive effect on their emotions and interpersonal encounters, and how well they understood others. Moreover, these benefits seemed to improve over time the more people practiced loving kindness meditation.

8. **May combat addiction**
In my meditation group, one member shared how meditation had helped them overcome their drug addiction. They said they'd meditated daily on the Serenity Prayer, which had really helped them become non-judgmental and accepting of themselves. They had also practised Metta meditation, which had supported them to be more compassionate towards themselves and forgive their past mistakes.

Research suggests that my friend's experiences are not an exception. Meditation helps you develop mental discipline, increasing your self-control and awareness of your triggers to break negative patterns of behaviour. Meditation can also support you to regulate your emotions and urges, redirect your attention when you experience a craving, and help you identify the cause of your addiction so you can work on the root cause.

One study involving 60 people suffering from alcoholism found that transcendental meditation helped them to lower their stress levels, bringing down the psychological distress they were experiencing, and reducing alcohol cravings and subsequent alcohol consumption after just three months. Another review looked into 14 studies and concluded that mindfulness meditation could help those with eating disorders by lowering the incidences of emotional and binge eating.

9. **Improves the quality of your sleep**
Almost half of us will suffer from insomnia at one time or another. Meditation is a good way of helping you relax and unwind to make it easier to get to sleep. Because meditation has a soothing, relaxing effect on the body, it can help you release tension so you can drift off. In addition, meditation may also help you refocus and still the inner chatter that keeps so many of us awake.

One study examined mindfulness-based meditation programs and concluded that meditation helped people stay asleep longer and reduced the severity of their insomnia in comparison to those in an unmedicated control group.

10. **Manages pain**
How you perceive pain is directly linked to your state of mind. If you're feeling stressed, pain levels rise.

THE POWER OF MEDITATION

Another person in my meditation group suffered from fibromyalgia and she told us that she'd first started meditating as a way to cope with the pain. She reported that although meditation didn't make her chronic pain go away, it made it more manageable by enabling her to stay in the moment and refocus her attention.

There is plenty of research to say that my friend's experience was more than just the placebo effect. One review of 38 studies found that mindfulness meditation was an effective way of reducing pain and improving the symptoms of depression, giving a better quality of life to people suffering from chronic pain. Another meta-analysis looked at studies covering almost 3,500 people and found that there was a clear connection between meditation and lowered levels of pain. While meditators and non-meditators might be dealing with the same cause of their pain, meditators had a stronger ability to cope with it and reported lower levels of pain.

11. Lowers blood pressure

High blood pressure is often known as the silent killer because you can suffer from it without experiencing any symptoms, but over time, its impact can be deadly. High blood pressure means the heart has to work harder to pump blood around the body, which can lead to decreased heart function. It can also contribute to atherosclerosis, which is a narrowing of the arteries that may cause heart attacks or strokes.

Meditation can reduce the strain on the heart, counteracting the damage caused by high blood pressure.

One meta-analysis of 12 studies covering almost 1,000 participants found that meditation could lower blood pressure, especially among older people and those already suffering from high blood pressure. What's more, another study found that this was true of a number of different types of meditation, meaning those with high blood pressure could choose the meditation method that was best for them.

While we don't yet fully understand the mechanisms by which meditation works, in this instance, one of the ways it controls blood pressure is by relaxing the nerve signals that co-ordinate heart function and blood vessel tension with the fight or flight response, which makes us more alert when under stress.

12. Boosts your immune system

Another surprising benefit of meditation is that it can improve your immune system. One study looked at blood samples taken before and after meditating. An analysis of the samples showed that there was greater activity of genes involved in regulating the immune response.

It should be pointed out that the meditators had been involved in eight days of 10-hour silent meditations, which would be difficult to recreate in the real world. While this retreat might not be a typical experience for most people, smaller experiments have suggested that short meditations on a daily basis may also improve an individual's immune response. What's more, attendees on that eight-day retreat were tested three months after the retreat ended. Their blood samples still showed an increased activity among immune-related genes.

Chapter Summary

Meditation has been scientifically proven to have a range of physiological and psychological benefits, including:

- Lower levels of stress
- Lower anxiety levels
- Improved emotional wellbeing
- Greater self-awareness
- Improved attention span
- Reduced impact of aging on memory
- Enhanced kindness
- Combatting addiction
- Improved quality of sleep
- Pain management
- Lower blood pressure
- Boosted immune system

CHAPTER TWO:

WHAT TO EXPECT WHEN YOU'RE MEDITATING

"With meditation, you become a sensitized superhero, completely in control, with endless possibilities at your fingertips."
—Tara Stiles

One of the hardest things for new meditators to grasp is how to know when you're actually meditating. There's nothing more frustrating than sitting there, wondering whether it's actually working, and realizing that the more you stress about whether you're really meditating, the further away you get from a meditative state.

First, it might be helpful to go into what meditation *is not.*

Meditation isn't daydreaming

When you meditate, you have a focus for your thoughts. That might be your breath, a mantra, an item, a visualization, and so on. During the meditation, you are aiming to keep your attention on that focus, which means that if you allow your thoughts to wander as they will, you're not meditating. Daydreaming might be a relaxing, fun thing to do, but it isn't true meditation.

Meditation isn't hypnosis

There are some similarities between the two practices. They both involve entering a trance state that results in similar brain wave patterns. However, there are also differences, which make them two distinct experiences.

Hypnosis is usually done under the guidance of a therapist, although it is possible to practice self-hypnosis. Conversely, meditation is usually done as a solitary practice, although it is possible to have someone guide you through the process.

Hypnosis involves consciously entering into a trance-like state of heightened awareness. We all naturally enter into a trance many times during the day. If you've ever had a moment when you lost track of time or couldn't remember doing something because you were so focused on something else, you were in a trance. Hypnosis deliberately places you into such a trance so that the therapist can communicate directly with the subconscious. During this trance, your breathing and heart-rate slow down and your brainwaves change. However, contrary to popular perception, you retain alertness and always have choice over what you do. You cannot be hypnotized into doing something you wouldn't ordinarily or willingly do.

While you are hypnotized, your hypnotherapist will guide you to gain control over any unwanted thoughts or processes so you can make changes to your behaviour or thinking. This is one of the main differences between meditation and hypnosis. Both offer benefits to the individual, but hypnosis tends to have a specific goal in mind, such as weight loss or quitting smoking. Working with a hypnotherapist, you can tackle the underlying programming to make permanent changes to achieve that goal.

In comparison, meditation has been shown to have multiple health benefits (which we covered in the previous chapter) but doesn't generally work with a specific outcome in mind. While one session of hypnosis can sometimes be enough to manifest these changes, meditation requires regular practice over a period of time for the benefits to show. These benefits may be subtle and easily missed unless an individual stops meditating for a while and notices the difference.

Meditation can be mindful, but it isn't mindfulness

You'll often hear the terms 'mindfulness' and 'meditation' being used interchangeably, but while there is an overlap, they aren't the same thing. For a start, mindfulness is a way of being, while meditation is something you do. John Kabat-Zinn, who created the Mindfulness-Based Stress Reduction (MBSR) program, says that mindfulness is "the awareness that arises through paying attention, on purpose, in the present moment, non-judgmentally."

In comparison, meditation involves focusing the mind on an object, thought, or activity, so while that might make it a mindful practice, you are consciously choosing what you think about in meditation, while mindfulness is more about observing what is without trying to change it.

Another way of looking at it is that mindfulness is about how you relate to yourself and your environment, while meditation is more about actively looking to change your state of mind.

Meditation is a mechanism for living more mindfully, although it isn't the only one. A 2008 study by Carmody & Baer found that people who practiced mindfulness meditation regularly, such as that taught through the MBSR program, were more capable of being mindful in their daily lives.

However, mindfulness can be pursued without meditating. A 2007 study by Thompson & Waltz found that mindfulness has a number of benefits to mental health, such as improved self-esteem and self-acceptance, which makes mindful living something worth doing. However, not everyone can or wants to meditate, so other treatments have been developed to support people to become more mindful, such as Dialectical Behavior Therapy (DBT). DBT helps people become more mindful without the requirement for any kind of formal practice. It means that people can enjoy a more mindful life even if they don't have time to meditate, struggle with meditation, or shouldn't be meditating due to their health.

Meditation is a formal practice. You have to set aside time and consciously do it, which can give you a break from the pressures of everyday life, but not everyone likes the idea of having to find time for yet another task on their to-do list.

Mindfulness can be part of a formal practice, but you can also do it informally throughout the day when opportunities arise. You can do mindful eating, mindful walking, mindful conversation, etc. In order to be mindful, all you have to do is choose to be mindful! Slow down, actively pay attention to the moment without judgment, and be fully present, and you'll find yourself being mindful.

Now you know what meditation is not...

...it's time to look at what meditation is and what you might experience when you're meditating.

There have been many studies that have shown that meditation changes your brainwaves while you're meditating. When we're asleep, our brain goes into a delta state. Scans have shown that there is little delta activity during meditation, so you aren't asleep when you're meditating.

The brain goes into a beta state while working on goal-oriented tasks, like planning an event or actively thinking about a problem. EEGs have shown that there is little beta activity when you're meditating.

During meditation, the brain experiences a lot of theta activity. These are the types of waves that are most common during deep relaxation. This occurs in conjunction with a lot of alpha activity in the posterior parts of the brain. Alpha waves are associated with wakeful rest.

While you might not be able to carry out a brain scan every time you're meditating, it's useful to be aware that your brain's activity is changing to reflect a time of active relaxation. When you first start meditating, you might be entering into this state without realizing it. One of the paradoxes of meditation is that thinking about whether you're meditating can pull you out of the meditative state. It's best to avoid trying to identify if you're meditating during your practice because this will make it harder for you to achieve that active, relaxed state. Rather, reflect on your experience afterwards, when you'll probably notice that while it might not have lasted for long, there were moments when you were in a meditative state. Over time, these moments will become longer as your brain becomes used to meditating.

You forget you're meditating

It's quite common to pay more attention to the clock and think about trying to meditate when you first start your practice. You might have set a timer for ten minutes and spend eight of those minutes opening one eye and sneaking a peek at how much longer you've got to wait...

If you're spending all your time wondering if you're actually meditating, you won't be able to go deep into your meditation (although if this is your experience, don't stress about it – you'll still have been meditating and you will get better with practice). If you find yourself forgetting that you're meditating and simply getting on with it, this is a good sign that you've been meditating!

Think about it – when you're struggling to go to sleep, if you lie there thinking about how you can't sleep, you're pretty much guaranteeing you won't sleep. But if you distract your mind by counting sheep, daydreaming, or reading, you'll find it easier to drift off. So if you let go of any worry about whether you're meditating properly and just get on with it, you'll find it much easier to enter into the meditative state.

Time moves differently

One very clear indicator of having meditated is losing track of time. Just as when you sleep, it doesn't feel like hours have passed, when you're meditating, time tends to pass faster. You might have meditated for ten minutes, but it only feels like two or three. When this happens, you'll know that you were in deep relaxation during your session.

Your body relaxes

When you meditate, you should have a straight posture, so your breathing is free and easy. You'll often find that when you finish your meditation, your back will slump and your head may hang forward, but you won't have noticed yourself moving. In fact, you may have felt like you were still as upright as when you started. This relaxation is perfectly natural and is why you might like to support your back from the start to help you maintain a good posture.

Your breathing slows

Regardless of whether you are doing a breath meditation or not, your breathing tends to become slower and shallower during meditation. You may even find that you stop breathing altogether for short periods. This reflects the body's activity. When you're engaged in physical activity, your breathing is heavy. When you're doing everyday chores, your breathing is normal. When you're relaxing with a book, your breathing slows a little. When you're asleep, your breathing slows down more. When you meditate, your breathing may become even slower than during sleep. It isn't something to worry about unless you start feeling uncomfortable, in which case you should stop meditating for that session.

Whether you experience any of the signs or not doesn't mean that you didn't get any benefit from your meditation. It doesn't matter how long you've been meditating. There will be times when you go deep into the process and times when you struggle to settle your mind. Even if you're meditating every day with the same technique, every session will be different, and you won't be able to predict what it will be like.

The only real difference between a new meditator and someone who has been doing it for a long time is that the former tends to place a value judgment on their meditations, seeing a deep meditation as 'good' and one filled with distractions as 'bad.' In comparison, when someone has been meditating for a while, they're able to leave judgment out of the equation. Their experience is simply their experience. This impartial attitude is what enables them to be more likely to enjoy a deep meditation because they've set aside any expectations about what 'should' happen and just let themselves be in the moment.

The most important thing is to be consistent. In the early stages of your meditation practice, you probably won't notice major changes (although you might), and it can take days, weeks, or months to start seeing the kinds of results you've read about. You need to persist, trusting that that those results *will* come, but probably when you least expect it. Meditate without putting any pressure on yourself. Ultimately, all meditations will be helping you and every time you meditate, you get one step closer to enjoying deep, effortless meditations.

In the next chapter, we'll be looking at what you can do to set yourself up for success by establishing a regular practice.

Chapter Summary

- Meditation isn't daydreaming.
- Meditation isn't hypnosis.
- Meditation isn't mindfulness, although it can be mindful.
- Your brainwaves change to theta and alpha waves during meditation.
- Paradoxically, you can tell you're meditating if you've forgotten that you're meditating.
- Time moves differently when you're in a meditative state.
- Your body relaxes during meditation.
- Your breathing naturally slows when you meditate, even if you're not doing a breath work meditation.
- It can take time to see the benefits of meditation, but persist and you'll get there.

CHAPTER THREE:

HOW TO ESTABLISH A MEDITATION PRACTICE

"A most useful approach to meditation practice is to consider it the most important activity of each day. Schedule it as you would an extremely important appointment, and unfailingly keep your appointment with the infinite."

—Roy Eugene Davis

As we covered in the previous chapter, consistency is one of the most important aspects to enjoying deep meditations. However, it can be difficult to get started. It can take anything from 18 to 254 days for someone to form a new habit. On average, it takes someone 66 days to make a new behaviour automatic, which means that you'll need to commit to meditating for at least two months and **consciously** follow through with that before meditation is seamlessly woven into your lifestyle.

You'll need to make a commitment to yourself that you're going to do this on a daily basis. While there is evidence to suggest that you don't *have* to meditate every day to experience the benefits, when you're just starting out, it's best to meditate every day so you can get into the habit. It's very easy to make an excuse for why you can't meditate one day, and when you've skipped that day, it's easier to give yourself the next day off too. Before you know it, you're coming up with reasons why you can't meditate most days. When you look back over your first month, you'll realize that you barely meditated at all, even though you feel like you did because you spent so much time thinking about why you couldn't meditate!

As a minimum, you should aim to meditate at least five times a week, so if you really, really must, you could give yourself weekends off, but if you're considering doing this, ask yourself why? Meditation is pleasurable and relaxing with so many benefits. (And if you don't think it's fun, you should consider changing the method you're using to something that works better for you.) Why wouldn't you want to give yourself a gift of time to yourself every single day?

There are a few things you can do to support yourself to establish a meditation routine. First of all, you should make it fun and comfortable. If you enjoy your meditation, you'll be motivated to do it again. If you don't, it'll be difficult to push yourself into repeating the experience.

Have a dedicated meditation space

Try and create a relaxing meditation space in your home. If you don't have an area you can set aside for your practice, consider getting some things you can use to create a soothing atmosphere, like incense, candles, or a meditation pillow. Having a specific place you go to for meditation will send a signal to your brain that you are going to consciously focus and relax, making it easier for you to get into the zone.

Make yourself comfortable

Whether you're able to set up a particular area for your meditation or not, you should always be comfortable when you do it. It's better to sit up than lie down when meditating. Because you are entering a state of deep relaxation, your mind may associate this with sleep. If you're lying down, you may find yourself regularly drifting off. This can be a sign you need the sleep, so let your experience be your experience...but sleeping isn't meditating.

However, the most important thing is that you find a position you can stay in for the length of your meditation with getting stiff, cramped, or restless. If you really can't meditate sitting up, lie down rather than attempt to push through physical discomfort.

Choose an upright posture that keeps your back straight and your airways clear. Your breathing should be natural and unhindered. You might like to support your lower back with cushions or you could get a meditation pillow or stool to help you maintain a good posture.

Start small

One of the main reasons people struggle to establish a meditation habit is because they're too ambitious when they get started. Meditation is a simple practice but that doesn't mean it's easy. If your mind isn't used to actively focusing on a single concept, it will fight against your attempts to control it, either by coming up with an array of intrusive thoughts or by making you physically uncomfortable so you fidget and twitch, breaking the mood. You'll find yourself constantly checking the clock, wondering how much longer you have to endure sitting still, and end up thinking you simply can't meditate.

If you start with short meditations, you'll feel like you accomplished something because you were able to focus for 2-3 minutes and you can gradually extend the amount of time as you get used to the experience. You are establishing a habit you'll enjoy for the rest of your life. There's no hurry to meditate for hours on end right from the start. You're not in competition with anyone, so enjoy the process. It's much better to have a couple of minutes of rest from your inner chatter than add to it by stressing about meditating for an arbitrary amount of time.

Schedule time in your diary and stick to it

Think about the things you do automatically every day, things like brushing your teeth, getting dressed, brushing your hair. It would be easy to not do these things. You don't *have* to brush your teeth if you don't want to. But you do it because you know it's good for you, and you remember to do it because you have a routine that includes teeth brushing as part of the process.

So it is with meditation. You'll find it easier to develop a habit of meditation if you include it in your routine at the same time every day. You might need to experiment to find the best time for you – you could meditate first thing in the morning before you get up, starting the day in a good mood knowing that you've already ticked your meditation box. If you're not a morning person, you might prefer to meditate last thing at night so you know that whatever time you go to bed, you'll definitely meditate, which will help you sleep better.

Alternatively, you might want to meditate at regular points during the day, such as during your commute to work (just don't meditate while driving), using meditation to keep you focused and refreshed.

Be kind to yourself

The more you can approach your meditating practice from a place of non-judgment, the easier it will be for you to enter a deep state. It's a misconception to believe you should be trying to empty your mind of any and all thought during a meditation. Your mind is thinking all the time and you should be working with that process rather than fighting it.

Recognize that your mind will fight your attempts to control it, wandering from thought to thought in an attempt to drag your attention away from your meditation. This might mean that you experience thoughts and feelings that may be difficult or distressing.

If this happens, acknowledge the thought without judgment before taking your attention back to the focus of your meditation. If this is difficult because the thought is so intrusive and persistent, you might like to thank your mind for drawing it to your attention and promise to come back to it later. Alternatively, you could imagine yourself putting the thought on a piece of paper and tying it to a balloon string so it flies away, or dropping the thought into a river and watching it float away like a leaf.

Keep a meditation journal

One of the most valuable tools I've found to support my meditation practice is my journal. This doesn't have to be anything extravagant. You could just get an ordinary notebook to record your thoughts. The main purpose here is to start documenting your experiences to build your self-awareness.

What you write in your journal is entirely up to you. There's no grade and no one ever needs to see it.

As a minimum, I'd advise recording the date, type of meditation, how long you meditated for, and a few sentences reflecting on your experience. Other pieces of information you might want to include are the time of day, your mood before and after meditating, and any insights you might have had.

You will quickly build up a valuable record of your meditation journey. Your journal will help keep you accountable. I know people who thought they were meditating almost every day only to look back over their journal and discover that they were barely managing to do it every few days.

It also helps to chart your progress. There will be days when you struggle to meditate and are tempted to give up. Your journal will help you see that you are progressing overall and the good days are gradually outnumbering the bad. This will help keep you motivated and give you the fortitude to keep going when you feel like it's a struggle.

You'll also find it easier to identify how meditation is helping you. The benefits can often be subtle and hard to see unless you're actively looking for them. Your journal will help you see that you're becoming calmer, less angry, less reactive, and more compassionate. If you're meditating because you want to improve your physical health, you might like to include details about that too, such as your blood pressure or resting heart rate. One person in my meditation classes wears a heart monitor and was delighted when she realized that her heart rate was consistently lowering during meditation to a healthier rate.

A few words of caution

I want to make you aware of some possible pitfalls associated with meditation. When you know the signs, you can take action to avoid any issues.

- **Don't expect too much too fast**

  It's tempting to think you'll find meditation easy because it's so deceptively simple. Then, when you find you struggle to maintain your focus, you decide you can't meditate and you give up.

  First of all, you should be aware that not all meditations suit all people. Meditation is simply the art of consciously inducing the same trance state your brain naturally enjoys as part of daily living. Everyone can meditate – if they find the right style of meditation for them. Later in this book we'll go into a wide range of meditation methods so you can experiment and find the ones that resonate with you and those that don't work for you right now.

  Give yourself time. You wouldn't expect to go to the gym and run 10 miles on the treadmill straightaway. You'd accept that it takes time to build up strength and stamina when you start a physical fitness program.

  It's the same with meditation. It'll take a while for you to build up your mind's strength and stamina, so go easy on yourself and keep your expectations low. That way, you'll be pleasantly surprised when you progress faster than you thought.

  In addition, don't expect meditation to be a quick fix for all your problems. Some people find that meditation gives fast results, but it's impossible to tell whether that will be the case for you. Meditation won't solve your problems; it just makes it easier for you to deal with them. Think about meditation as an important part of your self-care toolkit, one of many things you do to keep yourself healthy and less stressed.

- **Meditation isn't for everyone**

  Most of what you read about meditation will talk about how amazing it is and how great the benefits are. What isn't discussed so widely is the fact that some people shouldn't meditate.

  There are some types of meditation that aren't suitable for people with certain health conditions. If, for example, you suffer with a condition that affects your breathing, such as asthma or emphysema, you should avoid doing any kind of controlled breathing, and if you find yourself getting physically distressed during meditation, you should stop immediately.

  Likewise, there is evidence to suggest that some people suffering from mental health problems find that meditation makes things worse, not better. While most people find that meditation lifts their mood and reduces the symptoms of depression, for some, it makes things worse.

  After all, meditation involves going deep inside your mind. If your mind isn't a very positive place to be, it might not be the best thing to explore further until your mental health improves. For some individuals, meditation can exacerbate difficult thoughts and emotions, making your condition worse rather than better. There is also evidence to suggest that meditation might cause psychotic states in some individuals, so if you suffer from mental health conditions like schizophrenia, meditation may not be advised for you.

  If you have any concerns or questions, check with your medical professional to see if they think that meditation is a good option for you, and be aware that if you notice any worsening of symptoms, you should stop meditating immediately. Right now, you need to look for other methods of healing.

You may be able to go back to meditation if your health improves, but if you are one of those people who can't, try not to judge yourself or beat yourself up. Remember – your experience is your experience and there is no shame if meditation simply isn't right for you.

In the next chapter, we'll look at some quick, simple meditations you can do to get started and ease you into a daily practice.

Chapter Summary

- Meditate on a daily basis. The more consistent and regular you can be with your practice, the more you'll see the benefits. If you can't do it every day, aim to meditate at least five times a week.

- Have a dedicated meditation space to help get you in the zone.

- Wherever you meditate, treat your comfort as the number one priority. Meditation should be enjoyable, and that includes physical comfort.

- Start small, meditating for just a few minutes at a time, and gradually build up the amount of time you spend meditating.

- Schedule time in your diary for meditation and make it as non-negotiable as you would a business meeting or important appointment.

- Be kind to yourself. Practising non-judgment about your meditation experience will help you enjoy deeper meditations.

- Keep a meditation journal. Record your daily experiences to log your progress. This will help keep you accountable and motivated as you see the impact meditation has on your life.

- Don't put pressure on yourself when it comes to the quality of your meditations. It'll take time to train your mind to be able to focus for prolonged periods, so don't get frustrated if it takes you longer than expected to be able to go into a deep meditative state.

- Don't think meditation will fix all your problems. It will help you cope with the pressures of modern living, but it isn't a panacea.

- For a small minority of people, meditation will make their health problems worse, not better. For some, this is a temporary state and a sign you need to look for other ways of healing until you're ready to meditate. For others, meditation is just not an option for you and that's okay. If you notice any worsening of symptoms while meditating, stop immediately. Always consult a healthcare professional before meditating if you have any concerns.

CHAPTER FOUR:

———————————

FIRST STEPS IN MEDITATION

"Be here now. Be someplace later. Is that so complicated?"
—David M. Bader

Many people have a vision of meditation involving sitting in the lotus position for hours on end as you chant 'Om.' In fact, while this is one way of meditating, it is just as valid to do a quick meditation for as little as one minute.

When you know that you can do a really short meditation and it's as valid as a longer practice, it becomes easier to start weaving it into your day.

Research has shown that short meditations can be highly effective, so if you've been putting off starting your meditation practice because of time concerns, rest assured that even if you only do a few minutes, you'll still reap the benefits.

For example, research published in *Psychological Science* showed that just 15 minutes of meditation could improve decision-making abilities, while a study published in *Psychoneuroendocrinology* found that just three consecutive days of meditating for 25 minutes could lower stress levels. Yet another study published in the *Journal of the*

American Medical Association found that 30 minutes a day could improve the symptoms of anxiety and depression.

If even that seems too long, start shorter. Consistency is far more important than quantity. Starting with a short meditation helps you start and maintain the habit of meditation. If you tell yourself you're just going to do three minutes of meditation – and anyone can find three minutes to meditate – and you sit down and do it, you've already won, even if you don't feel like your meditation was particularly deep. The very act of getting started is a huge step forward and you can gradually extend the length of your meditation when you want. Work to your timetable and don't worry about whether you can meditate as long as other people.

A shorter, more focused meditation is going to be more effective than sitting for longer with your mind drifting all over the place. Many people find the start of their meditation to be the most focused. As their meditation progresses, if something happens to snap them out of the trance state, it can be difficult, if not impossible, to get back into the zone. You might like to note in your journal if this happens – you can use this to track how long you're able to hold your focus. You will notice that the length increases over time, even if it doesn't feel like you're improving.

If you need, give yourself permission to start small and not put any pressure on yourself for how long you should meditate. You can do the meditations in this chapter in as little as a minute. They're a good place to start and prove to yourself that meditation doesn't have to be challenging or a marathon of staring at the walls.

Connect with the feeling of your breath

One of the simplest meditations is to take a moment to tune into your breath. Without trying to control it in any way, just observe the feelings and sensations associated with the flow of breath. You might like to focus your attention on your nostrils and feeling the air entering and leaving your body. Or you could follow the flow of breath right down to your lungs and feel it moving through your body. Or you could watch your belly rise and fall with the breath.

It doesn't really matter where you place your attention as long as you choose something connected with your breath to focus on and allow yourself a few moments to press pause on everyday life.

The beauty of this meditation is that you can do it anywhere, any time (although as previously mentioned, don't meditate while you're driving or doing anything that requires your full attention for safety reasons, such as operating machinery). You can even do it around other people – nobody will know that you're meditating if you take a few moments to observe your breath, and it's a great way to ground and centre yourself.

Take three clearing breaths

This meditation is exactly what you'd think it would be – the simple act of taking three breaths. You can do this any time during the day. It's a good way of letting go of any tension so it doesn't build up.

Take a moment to turn your attention fully to your breath. Inhale as deeply as you can through your nose and then exhale through your mouth. Make the exhale as long as you can and feel free to make a noise as you do so. You might like to sigh or let out a lovely 'haaa.'

Do this for three breath cycles and then go about your day.

Watch your thoughts

Another short meditation involves sitting with your thoughts without judgment. Remember – meditation is not about clearing your mind. It's more about what you choose to fill it.

Take a moment to connect with your breath. You might like to take a few deep inhalations, holding for a moment, then slowly exhaling to bring yourself into the moment. As with the previous meditation, observe how the breath feels as it flows through your body.

When you're ready, allow thoughts to come. You might like to label the thoughts with the emotion they evoke or note whether they're positive or negative.

This is a nice way to check in with your current state of mind and learn to simply be without criticism or judgment.

Scan your body

A body scan meditation is a good way to tune in to your body. Our bodies communicate a wealth of information, but we don't always notice because we've become so detached from ourselves. A body scan allows you to observe your current state of being, supporting you to notice if you're holding any stress or tension in a particular area and send love with the breath to that area.

Begin by making yourself comfortable, either lying or sitting down. Bring your attention into your body. You can close your eyes if that's comfortable for you.

Take a few deep breaths. As you inhale, observe the breath flowing into your body and as you exhale, feel yourself becoming more and more relaxed.

When you're ready, turn your attention to your feet. Notice how they feel against the floor or wherever they are resting.

Notice your legs and how they feel.

Notice your back and how it feels resting against the thing supporting you.

Bring your attention into your stomach area. If your stomach is tense or tight, let it soften. Take a breath and as you exhale, breathe out any tension.

Notice your hands. Are they tense? See if you can allow them to soften.

Notice your arms. Are they leaning against anything? How does that feel? Feel any sensations in your arms.

Move your attention up to your shoulders. Let your shoulders soften and relax.

Notice your neck and throat. Let them be soft. Let yourself relax even further.

Soften your jaw. Let your face be soft and relaxed.

Now take a moment to observe your whole body. Take one more breath as you run your attention from the top of your head to the tips of your toes. If there are any areas of stress or tension, breathe love into those parts of your body.

Now be aware of your whole body as best you can from head to toe. Take a breath. And when you're ready, open your eyes.

Tune into your senses

This is a lovely mindful meditation you can do at any time to bring you back into the present moment. You can make it as quick or as long as you like – set a timer so you spend the same amount of time with each sense, and repeat the meditation, cycling through each sense as many times as you like. It really is up to you how you work with this meditation.

A good starting point is to spend a minute with each sense, giving it your full attention.

Close your eyes and turn your focus to your hearing. What's the loudest sound you can hear? What's the quietest? How many different sounds can you notice? Spend some time listening to the world around you without judgment or trying to label the sounds you hear.

Now turn your attention to your sense of smell. Can you smell anything? Are there any strong smells? Any subtle scents?

Now turn your attention to your sense of taste. Can you taste anything in your mouth? Maybe an aftertaste of something you ate or drank earlier?

Nowturn your attention to your sense of touch. What can you feel against your body? How do your clothes feel? Is your body resting against a chair, a bed, the floor? What does that feel like?

Now gently open your eyes and gaze around you. Observe the colours you can see. Is there one in particular that jumps out at you? Can you see any shadows? Does the light change how things look? Do you notice anything you haven't spotted before?

When you're ready, bring your awareness of your senses back to normal.

Chapter Summary

- Research has shown that even short meditations can benefit you.
- Start small, with just a few minutes of meditation, but do it every day.
- Track your progress in your journal so you can see how your focus is improving.
- If you still find the idea of meditating daunting, reassure yourself with the fact you can meditate for as little as a minute.
- Connect with the feeling of your breath and observe its movement in your body.

- Take three clearing breaths anytime during the day to release tension and prevent it from building up.
- Watch your thoughts as they arise to check in with your current state of mind. You might like to label the thoughts according to emotion or whether they're positive or negative.
- Do a body scan to tune in to your body and build a stronger connection with it.
- A simple mindful meditation is to focus on each one of your senses in turn, observing how you're experiencing the current moment without judgment.

CHAPTER FIVE:

BREATHWORK

"If you have time to breathe, you have time to meditate. You breathe when you walk. You breathe when you stand. You breathe when you lie down."

—Ajahn Amaro

There's a reason we tell someone to take deep breaths when they're stressed, angry, or frustrated. It's a quick and easy way to bring yourself back into the moment and release tension, calming yourself down.

One of the simplest forms of meditation to base your practice on is working with your breath. After all, everyone breathes! Yet not all of us breathe fully or properly, depriving ourselves of this simple, essential source or rejuvenation.

There are countless ways to work with your breath. Which one you choose will depend on what you hope to achieve, as well as what you find the most pleasurable. Remember – you want your meditation experience to be as positive and enjoyable as possible so you actively want to continue with it rather than seeing it as a chore.

Not everyone gets on with breathing meditations – some personality types find it a little too passive, and struggle to maintain focus. The only way you can know if you like it is to do it!

Also remember that meditation shouldn't cause you any distress or discomfort. If you have any conditions that affect your breathing, you should consult a medical professional before starting with breath work. Likewise, even if you don't have any health problems but you find yourself feeling uncomfortable while you're working with a breathing meditation, stop and try a different way. We'll be covering plenty of other techniques in this book, so you have plenty of choices.

How long you do these meditations is entirely up to you. I suggest you set a timer for 3-5 minutes when you first start and gradually extend the amount of time as you become more comfortable with the techniques.

Observing the breath

Probably the simplest form of meditation is to observe the breath. This is sometimes known as the "reset breath" or "the breath that brings you back to the present." According to a 2018 study published in the *Journal of Cognitive Enhancement,* long-term practice of this breath meditation can improve your ability to maintain focus and slow the progress of age-related cognitive decline.

Make yourself comfortable somewhere you won't be disturbed, either sitting or standing. Make sure your upper body is straight so your breath can flow freely without any disruption. Close your eyes or soften your gaze, whatever is more comfortable to you. Now tune in to the cycles of your breath, feeling the rise and fall of your belly. Treat each breath as an individual experience, observing its flow. You might like to keep your attention at your nostrils, feeling the breath enter your body. You might like to follow the journey of your breath down into your lungs and back up again.

Whatever way you choose to watch your breath, when your mind wanders, as soon as you become aware of your loss of focus, gently bring your attention back to the breath again.

Counting your breaths

Some people struggle to simply watch their breath. If this is you, you might find this technique more appropriate.

As you inhale, silently count in your mind: One.

Exhale.

With your next inhale, silently count in your mind: Two.

Exhale.

With your next inhale, silently count in your mind: Three.

Exhale.

Continue this process until you've counted to 10. Then go back to one and start all over again.

A variation on this technique is to count the exhale as well: Inhale *one,* exhale *one,* inhale *two,* exhale *two,* etc. You can also count up to 10 and then back down again. Experiment to find which version works for you.

If you lose track of how far you've counted, don't worry. Just go back to one and start again. Likewise, if you find that you've gone past 10 and you're counting in the teens or even twenties, don't worry. Just go back to one and start again.

Recharging your energies with your breath

If you're feeling under the weather or you really need a holiday but you can't take time off, you can use your breath to refresh and rejuvenate yourself.

Make yourself comfortable and take a moment to connect with your breath. Observe its flow without judgment or trying to control it in anyway. Notice whether it's fast or slow, shallow or deep. Now you can start using the breath to refuel yourself. As you inhale, feel your body drawing in the breath of life through your nostrils and down to your lungs, through to the rest of your body. Feel your body filling with that beautiful drink of breath. During your inhalation, allow your chest to expand fully, your shoulders pulling back, creating more space in your chest. Feel your rib cage opening, your abdomen inflating.

When you're ready, release the breath as slowly as you can and watch how your body feels following that breath of life.

Repeat this cycle, each time letting the breath become slower and longer, refreshing and relaxing you more and more. With each inhalation, draw in peace, joy, and love, and with each exhalation, release more and more stress and tension until you are nothing but calm and happiness.

Diaphragm breathing

This type of meditation has its origins in the kundalini tradition. Your diaphragm is located at the bottom of your lungs and plays a major role in the process of breathing. Not everyone breathes effectively with their diaphragm, so this meditation can help you how to target it more, strengthening its ability to move the air in, around, and out of your body. This enables you to take in more air with each breath, making it good for people who suffer from chronic obstructive pulmonary disease (COPD) to provide some relief from shortness of breath and improve circulation. If you want to use it for this purpose, you might like to do this as often as 3-4 times every day for 5-10 minutes per session.

Sit or lie down, making sure your upper body is erect so the air can flow freely. Put one hand on your upper chest and the other on your belly just below your rib cage. Breathe in slowly and deliberately and allow your stomach to push your hand up. Try to keep the hand on your chest as still as possible, while you focus on moving the hand on your belly. Aim to take long, deep breaths that completely fill your lungs rather than shallow, fast-moving ones.

Zhuanqi or breathing until the breath is soft

This is a Taoist meditation that is similar to diaphragm breathing. Its purpose is to unite your breath and mind by keeping your attention on your breath until it is soft and quiet.

Sit comfortably with your upper body erect so you can breathe freely. Unfocus your gaze, looking gently at the point of your nose. Place your right hand on your belly and your left on your chest. Inhale deeply and observe which hand moves more and in which direction. Exhale slowly and repeat the process for the length of your meditation. Your ultimate aim is for the hand on your abdomen to be moving more than the one on your chest, going in and out rather than up and down.

Alternate nostril breathing

Alternate nostril breathing involves controlling your breath by breathing in through one nostril while keeping the other closed. In a 2017 study published in *Medical Science Monitor Basic Research,* this specific type of meditation lowered blood pressure, reducing the systolic blood pressure in participants after just 18 minutes. It also increased their ability to focus, enabling them to carry out a vigilance task in less time than the control group. Other research in the *International*

Journal of Psychophysiology, found that alternate nostril breathing can balance the left and right hemispheres of the brain.

Make yourself comfortable, sitting upright with your right hand resting on your knee. Use your left thumb to gently close your left nostril. Inhale slowly through your right nostril, then close your right nostril with your ring finger. Pause for a moment, then exhale through your left nostril. Inhale slowly through your left nostril, then close your left nostril with your thumb. Pause for a moment, then exhale slowly through your right nostril. Continue this for the length of your meditation. Ideally, you should do this meditation for 15-20 minutes, so if that's a little out of reach for you at the moment, wait until you've built up your ability to focus before trying this form of meditation.

Box breathing

This form of breath meditation is known to be used by the United States Navy Seals for its powerful ability to lower stress. It is sometimes known as 4x4 breathing, 4-4-4-4 breathing, equal breathing, or square breathing. You can use this technique any time you're feeling under pressure to bring down cortisol levels and lower your blood pressure, relieving the physical symptoms of stress. It can also help trigger the relaxation response, activating the parasympathetic nervous system to calm you down.

The technique is very simple. Make yourself comfortable, with your upper body erect. Breathe out slowly, emptying your lungs.

Inhale through your nose as you count to four in your mind.

Hold your breath as you count to four.

Exhale for another count of four.

Hold your breath again for a count of four.

Repeat this cycle as many times as you need.

Remember that this should be a comfortable, relaxing experience. If you find yourself feeling short of breath or any kind of discomfort, stop using this technique and allow your breath to return to normal.

Let your body be your guide. Count as fast or as slowly as is comfortable for you.

Intermittent breath retention

This Hindu meditation involves holding your breath following the inhale and exhale. This gentle pause should be shorter than your inhales and exhales. According to a study in the *Indian Journal of Medical Research,* briefly holding your breath can increase the amount of oxygen your body consumes by up to 56%. Another study published in the *Indian Journal of Physiology and Pharmacology* found that intermittent breath retention may help avoid metabolism issues as a result of the rate your body uses and burns oxygen.

Sit comfortably with your upper body erect so your breath can flow freely. Exhale as much as you can through your mouth. Close your mouth and inhale slowly through your nose until your lungs are completely full. Hold this air for a count of 3-5 seconds and slowly exhale. When you have emptied your lungs, hold your breath for 3-5 seconds before inhaling deeply. Continue this cycle for as long as you wish.

Create space with your breath

If you're feeling like your body is filled with tension and pent-up energy, this meditation is a good one to breathe more space back into your body and get those energies flowing again.

Sit upright in a chair with your back straight, or you might prefer to stand for this one, making sure you don't lock your knees.

Turn your attention to your feet and feel the sensation of the vast expanse of the earth beneath you. As you do, say to yourself, *I claim my space.*

Breathe in and as you do, draw up energy from that space, using the breath to send it all around your body.

Exhale, and with your out breath let go of any excess tension, creating even more space within your body.

Continue to draw energy up through your feet with every inhalation and send it anywhere in your body where you can sense tension or stress. As you do, say in your mind, *I claim space for my [body part].*

Repeat this pattern for as long as you need.

A nice variation on this meditation is to look out over a wide-open space. If you have beautiful views from your window, gaze outside, or take a trip out to the countryside. If this isn't possible, you can find a pretty natural landscape on the internet or simply visualize being beside the ocean or sitting in a meadow or forest. As you breathe in, feel your breath matching the expanse of the view in front of you. Bring that space into you, sending it all over your body.

Sending the breath through your body

This meditation can take you into a deep state of relaxation. It's a good one to do lying down and you can use it to help you enjoy a good night's sleep. You can also do it sitting or even standing – whatever feels right for you.

Make yourself comfortable and tune in to your breath.

As you inhale, feel the start of your breath in your pelvis, traveling up the front of your body, all the way up to the top of your head. As you exhale, see the breath travel down the back of your spine to your pelvis, right back to where you started. You'll naturally draw the breath back up to the top of your head with your next inhalation and send it back down your spine.

Continue this cycle for as long as you like – it can be incredibly pleasurable to allow the breath to flow in this way and you'll feel wonderfully relaxed after this relaxation.

Healing breath to connect with your body

If you're feeling a negative emotion, such as stress, tension, anxiety, or fear, this is a good meditation to help calm you down.

Make yourself comfortable, close your eyes, and turn your attention to your body. Ask yourself, *Where in my body am I feeling emotion?*

If you're not used to tuning in to your body, you may struggle with this and that's okay. Simply observe your body. You might feel tension in your stomach, a constriction in your throat, pressure on your shoulders, a tightness in your jaw, strange sensations around your heart. However you feel, notice it without judgment.

Put your hands somewhere you're feeling an emotion. In your mind, ask yourself, *What do I need to hear? What do I need to remember?* Sit with any answers that come up. Don't discount anything you get – let your experience be your experience. It's all valuable information.

As the answers come, reinforce the messages by massaging them into your body. You might like to give yourself a soothing tummy rub or reassuring hug.

You can repeat this process as many times as you like, working your way around the body as you reconnect with yourself and open up communication with the wisdom of your body and mind.

Using the breath to connect with the universe

Sometimes we can feel lonely or isolated. This meditation can help reassure you that you are never truly alone. We are all connected to the universe.

Make yourself comfortable somewhere you won't be disturbed. Inhale deeply and as you do, feel gratitude for this new breath. This wonderful breath, which is coming through your nostrils, traveling down your throat, filling your heart and lungs with nurturing air. Sense how this breath travels through every single cell of your body, filling you with vital oxygen and replenishing your energies. This is a gift from the universe, sending you love and peace with every inhalation.

As you breathe out, remember that a miraculous transformation is occurring. That oxygen you've inhaled has been turned into carbon dioxide, which is *your* gift back to the world around you. You are breathing out the vital nutrients that plants need to grow.

Every inhalation is a gift from the universe to you.

Every exhalation is gift from you to the universe.

You are an essential part of the process of life. You help keep the world turning.

Sit with this realization for as long as you need.

We're all breathing all the time. It's estimated the human body goes through about 22,000 breaths every day. Exploring this essential process can lead to deeply profound meditative experiences. It enables us to press pause on the busyness of modern living and spend a moment peacefully reconnecting with ourselves.

Working with the breath can also teach a powerful lesson about going with the flow. The only constant in life is change, yet there are also regular, predictable cycles. Spending time with your breath can help you find your inner strength and learn from the flexibility found in its flow.

However, not everyone enjoys or connects well with breath meditations. So in the next chapter, we're going to look at a different style of meditating: loving kindness meditation.

Chapter Summary

- Working with your breath is a quick and easy way to ground yourself in the present moment and let go of any stress or tension.
- There are numerous ways to work with the breath. It's worth trying out several different types to find the ones you like the most.
- If breath work causes you any physical stress or discomfort, stop doing it and try a different way.
- You do not have to do a breath meditation for long. Try starting by setting a timer for 3-5 minutes to begin, and then slowly extend the length of your meditation.
- Some of the most popular types of breath meditation include:
  - Observing the breath
  - Counting breaths
  - Recharging your energies with your breath
  - Diaphragm breathing
  - Zhuanqi, or breathing until the breath is soft
  - Alternate nostril breathing
  - Box breathing
  - Intermittent breath retention
  - Create space with your breath
  - Sending the breath through your body
  - Healing breath to connect with your body
  Using the breath to connect with the universe
- It's estimated that humans breathe 22,000 times every day. Working with this simple, natural bodily function can result in some incredibly profound experiences, as well as having a positive impact on your mind and body.

CHAPTER SIX:

LOVING KINDNESS OR METTA MEDITATION

"It is indeed a radical act of love just to sit down and be quiet for a time by yourself."
—Jon Kabat-Zinn

So many people struggle with being kind and compassionate to themselves. Their self-talk is filled with negative chatter and self-criticism. And while they're happy to be gentle and loving towards others, for some reason, they find it hard to believe they're just as worthy of compassion.

If you recognize yourself in this description, loving kindness meditation – or Metta meditation – could be the perfect practice for you. It is no less than the ultimate expression of profoundly selfless love towards others – but also yourself.

'Metta' is a Pali word meaning benevolence, friendship, affection and kindness. This type of meditation brings together the four main qualities of love – friendship, appreciation & joy, compassion, and equanimity.

As with all forms of meditation, loving kindness meditation should be practiced without judgment or expectation. It is a process that encourages you to be in the moment, enjoying it for what it is, regardless of experience.

One very important aspect of loving kindness meditation is that we always start with sending loving kindness to ourselves. To paraphrase the inimitable RuPaul, if you can't love yourself, how can you love anyone else? When we give without allowing ourselves to receive anything in return, it ultimately leads to burnout. As they say on flights, put on your own oxygen mask before you try to help anyone else. You might think you're doing the right thing by always putting others first, but you can't truly support anyone else if you're neglecting yourself. Eventually you'll crash and burn.

As you develop your ability to accept love and kindness through the practice of this meditation, you'll also notice an enhanced ability to show yourself compassion, a longer attention span, and a deep connection to your emotions, enabling you to keep your thoughts and actions in balance.

Loving kindness has many advantages:

- It is fully inclusive. It can be practised regardless of age, personality type, or circumstance. No matter what your situation, you can adapt loving kindness meditation to suit your needs.
- It is a simple form of meditation that can be practiced anywhere, any time. You can adjust the length to suit the time you have available and still feel its benefits.
- It does not have any strings attached. There is no obligation on the meditator to do anything as a result of the meditation, and it does not induce self-indulgent sentimentality. All you need to do is be in the moment and focus on the process.

- The benefits of loving kindness meditation are long-lasting, potentially staying with the meditator for a lifetime. People who practise this form of meditation on a regular basis find it to be a good way of understanding themselves better, learning more about their motivations, and developing their ability to be empathetic.

Research surrounding loving kindness meditation

There is a wealth of evidence to support the tangible benefits of loving kindness meditation, whether practised by itself or in conjunction with other forms of therapy and treatment. A study by Grossman and Van Dam in 2001 showed that it could enhance brain functions related to emotional regulation, stress management, and the functionality of the immune system.

Lutz et al. (2009) found that loving kindness meditation could be used as part of cognitive and behavioural treatment. Neuroimaging studies showed that it could regulate the function of the limbic system, the part of the brain that deals with processing emotions and empathy.

Loving kindness meditation has its roots in Buddhism, and traditionally Buddhists hold that this particular form of meditation is a gateway to cultivating happiness, appreciation, contentment, and self-acceptance. It supports us to focus on our positive emotions, creating profound shifts in thinking and attitudes.

Studies carried out on Tibetan monks with over 10,000 hours of experience in loving kindness meditation showed that they had atypically secure neural circuits associated with empathy and self-awareness. They also had higher levels of self-contentment and inner joy when compared to non-meditators or meditators who worked with other forms of meditation.

Other studies specifically looking at loving kindness meditation found that during a loving kindness meditation, the insula and parietal juncture, the parts of the brain linking perception and emotions, were activated faster than with other types of meditation. These are important areas in the brain because they support us to feel and express our emotions in a healthy way, which goes some way towards explaining why loving kindness creates sensations of pure happiness and self-love.

The benefits of loving kindness meditation

Metta meditation involves repeating positive, kind phrases to yourself, such as *may you be happy, may you know love, may you be healthy, may you be strong.* This process supports you to quickly develop a strong sense of self-worth. All you need to do is spend a few moments feeling appreciation and gratitude first for yourself and then for others. This practice has a long-term influence on your mind and body, bringing with it an empowering sense of positivity. Some of the documented benefits of loving kindness meditation include:

Lower levels of self-criticism

It is difficult to criticize or harm yourself when you're in the depths of a loving kindness meditation. This process stills your inner critic, making you more self-accepting and understanding of yourself.

Greater positive emotions

Studies carried out by Kok et al. (2013) found that the regular practice of loving kindness meditation could increase your vagal tone, a physiological indicator of subjective wellbeing.

The positive feelings created by loving kindness meditation have an impact from the inside out, attracting more positive experiences, enhancing your quality of life and making you feel more content.

Fewer self-destructive thoughts

Research carried out by Fredrickson, Coffey, Finkel, Cohn & Pek (2008) found that seven weeks of loving kindness meditation brought with it increased feelings of joy, gratitude, hope and compassion. Participants with suicidal tendencies or borderline personality traits reported a large reduction in self-harming urges and experienced an overall reduction in their negative symptoms.

Lower levels of pain

Tonelli et al. (2014) and Carson et al. (2005) did some pilot studies on patients suffering from chronic back pain and migraines. They found that when patients did a loving kindness meditation for as little as 2-5 minutes per day, they enjoyed markedly lower feelings of pain and were able to go about their daily lives with more ease.

Increased resilience

A study by Kearney et al. (2013) involving people suffering from PTSD found that when they regularly practised loving kindness meditation and self-compassion, they experienced less trauma and fewer flashbacks. Groups that were given loving kindness scripts during their therapy were able to get back to work sooner than those who were taken through other guided instructions.

Quicker recovery

Studies looking at people with schizophrenia and bipolar disorders (Johnson et al., 2011) found they experienced significantly fewer negative symptoms, including hallucinations and delusions, when they practiced loving kindness meditation, either individually or in a group setting. In addition to feeling more positive and having fewer symptoms, it was also found that they were more positive in their judgment of those they lived or worked with.

Long-lasting positive impact

Studies examining the after-effects of loving kindness meditation found that people who went to sessions involving this form of meditation continued to feel more positive and self-motivated for as long as 15 months after they finished the course. When compared with other types of meditation or self-help tools, loving-kindness supported participants to feel more affection and empathy towards strangers, as well as helping them build better connections at work (Seppala and Gross, 2008.)

The basics of loving kindness meditation

With so many benefits, there really isn't any reason *not* to incorporate loving kindness into your meditation practice. Who wouldn't want to experience more inner peace, happiness, love, self-awareness, and affection? It's a very flexible, simple way of meditating that can be tailored to your personal needs, whether they be personal, professional, or spiritual.

As with any meditation, there are no right or wrong ways to practice loving kindness meditation, only **your** way. However, there are a few foundational concepts you'll want to incorporate:

- Make sure you practice loving kindness regularly, whether it be daily, weekly, or monthly. Regular meditation is key to experiencing the full range of benefits, so ideally you should aim to be doing it at least once a week. You might like to have a full loving kindness meditation, which takes 20 minutes, and then do a little bit of loving kindness every day by repeating your affirmations.

- Make sure you're comfortable while you do your meditation. Choose a posture that allows the breath to flow freely and you'll be able to maintain for the length of your meditation. You can sit or lie down, use a chair, meditation cushion, or stool. Whatever makes it easy for you to relax into the moment. Wear comfortable clothes that don't restrict you in any way. You might like to lower the lighting and minimize noise if possible. Eliminate distractions – switch off your phone for the duration of your meditation, turn off the TV or radio, and put away your devices. You are giving yourself the gift of the present moment, so don't do anything to diminish that gift.

- No matter how long or short your meditation, you should always start by sending loving kindness to yourself **first**. In fact, when you begin with this form of meditation, you might like to solely work with yourself before you start to include other people in your practice. As you become more comfortable with this meditation, bring in friends, family, colleagues, strangers, and even people you find problematic.

- You will need to choose some positive affirmations to use in your meditation. These should be in the present tense and always start with the words "May I..." Pick some phrases that work best for you – I'll give you some examples in a moment. Depending on what's going on in your life at the moment, you might find it harder to use some phrases. For instance, if you've just ended a relationship, you might struggle to use the phrase *May I be loved.* Alternatively, you might find that a comforting affirmation to use. It very much depends on your personal preferences. All that matters is that you have some blessings you can send to yourself and others, and that these are things you feel comfortable accepting or wish to see more of in your life.

- As with breath meditation, start small and gradually build up your practice. Start with just a couple of minutes and see how you get on before lengthening the amount of time you spend meditating.

- As you say the blessings to yourself, try to fully embrace the meaning of the words. So, if you're saying, *May you be happy,* try to embody that emotion. If you're saying, *May you be safe,* try to connect with how safe you feel.

- Journal your experiences with this meditation. This will help you develop even more self-awareness as you reflect on how easy or hard you found it and any insights that arose during the session. It's also fascinating to watch how the practice becomes easier over time as you become more comfortable with accepting love.

Suggestions for your loving kindness meditation

While I'll be providing you with a script later in this chapter, which you can follow as written, you will probably find your meditation to be most effective if you use phrases that specifically resonate with you. Choose some from the list below or feel free to come up with your own:

- May I/he/she/they be happy.
- May I/he/she/they be healthy.
- May I/he/she/they be accepting and forgiving.
- May I/he/she/they know peace.
- May I/he/she/they be safe.
- May I/he/she/they love unconditionally.
- May I/he/she/they have everything they want and need.
- May I/he/she/they live in the present moment.
- May I/he/she/they always know love.

Sample loving kindness meditation script

You can adapt this script for your own purposes, replacing the blessings with ones more appropriate for you. All loving kindness starts with yourself, and as you begin this practice, you might like to simply focus on the part of the meditation that is directed towards yourself and incorporate other people as you progress on your journey.

As you build on your practice, start to include people who are farther away from your immediate circle. You can do this gradually, adding in one new person with every meditation.

A suggested order for people in your loving kindness meditation could be:

- Yourself
- Someone you love
- Someone you know but not very well, e.g., a colleague or sales assistant
- A stranger you've seen but never spoken to
- Someone with whom you are currently in conflict

The process for working with each person is the same: you hold them in your mind and heart as you repeat your chosen affirmations and send loving kindness in their direction. You might like to record yourself reading the script to guide yourself through the meditation, so you don't have to worry about what you're supposed to be doing next.

Make yourself comfortable somewhere you won't be disturbed, sitting with your back straight and your eyes closed. Alternatively, you can keep your eyes open, but soften your gaze so you aren't looking at anything in particular.

Take a moment to connect with your breath, letting it flow without judgment or trying to control it in any way.

When you are ready, repeat your affirmations to yourself: *May I be happy, may I be healthy, may I be safe. May I be happy, may I be healthy, may I be safe. May I be happy, may I be healthy, may I be safe.*

Sit for a moment, observing how your affirmations make you feel. Reflect on the words and the response they evoke in you. Do this without judgment, simply allowing your experience to be your experience.

When you are ready, think of someone you love, someone you are close to, someone who has treated you well, either now or in the past. Hold them in your mind and heart as you silently repeat your affirmations: *May they be happy, may they be healthy, may they be safe. May they be happy, may they be healthy, may they be safe. May they be happy, may they be healthy, may they be safe.*

Sit for a moment, sending feelings of loving kindness in the direction of your loved one.

When you are ready, think of someone you know but you aren't close to, someone you maybe see on a regular basis, like a colleague, neighbour, or sales assistant. Hold them in your mind and heart as you silently repeat your affirmations: *May they be happy, may they be healthy, may they be safe. May they be happy, may they be healthy, may they be safe. May they be happy, may they be healthy, may they be safe.*

Sit for a moment, sending feelings of loving kindness in the direction of your acquaintance.

When you are ready, think of a stranger, someone who you've maybe seen recently but have never spoken to. Hold them in your mind and heart as you silently repeat your affirmations: *May they be happy, may they be healthy, may they be safe. May they be happy, may they be healthy, may they be safe. May they be happy, may they be healthy, may they be safe.*

Sit for a moment, sending feelings of loving kindness in the direction of this stranger.

When you are ready, think of someone you are in conflict with, either now or in the past. Maybe this person has hurt you badly. Maybe you're no longer in contact with them. Hold them in your mind and heart as you silently repeat your affirmations: *May they be happy, may they be healthy, may they be safe. May they be happy, may they be healthy, may they be safe. May they be happy, may they be healthy, may they be safe.*

Sit for a moment, sending feelings of loving kindness in the direction of the person who has upset you.

Now send loving kindness all around the world. In your mind, say: *May we all be happy, may we all be healthy, may we all be safe. May we all be happy, may we all be healthy, we all be safe. May we all be happy, may we all be healthy, may we all be safe.*

Sit for a moment, sending feelings of loving kindness in the direction of your acquaintance.

Know that someone somewhere is doing a loving kindness meditation right now, sending as much love and compassion in your direction as you are sending to them. Take a moment to bask in this beautiful feeling of connection.

When you are ready, open your eyes.

It is a good idea to journal your experiences as soon as you've finished meditating while the feelings are still fresh in your mind. You'll notice that the more you do this meditation, the more you'll naturally start feeling more affectionate and loving towards yourself and others, bringing the compassion you experience during your meditation into your daily life.

Not everyone finds it easy to do loving kindness meditations. If you feel it is too overwhelming for you right now, work with a different kind and come back to it when you're ready. There are still plenty of meditations for you to work with.

In the next chapter, we're going to delve into mantra meditations and chanting, some of my favourite types of meditation!

Chapter Summary

- Many people find it hard to show kindness and compassion towards themselves. Practising loving kindness meditations can help you to be gentler and more understanding towards yourself as well as others.

- Loving kindness meditation is suitable for all ages, personality types, or circumstances.

- You can do short loving kindness meditations for a few minutes whenever you feel the need to be more compassionate towards yourself.

- The benefits of loving kindness meditation have been shown to be long-lasting, even when someone no longer practises it.

- It does not have any strings attached. There is no obligation on the meditator to do anything as a result of the meditation, and it does not induce self-indulgent sentimentality. All you need to do is be in the moment and focus on the process.

- The benefits of loving kindness meditation are ongoing, potentially staying with the meditator for a lifetime. People who practise this form of meditation on a regular basis find it to be a good way of understanding themselves better, learning more about their motivations, and developing their ability to be empathetic.
- There has been a wealth of research carried out into loving kindness meditation. Scientifically proven benefits include:
  ○ Enhanced brain functions associated with emotional regulation
  ○ Better stress management
  ○ Improved immune system
  ○ Improved function of the limbic system, responsible for processing emotions and empathy
  ○ Higher levels of self-contentment, empathy, self-awareness, and inner joy
  ○ Lower levels of self-criticism
  ○ Fewer self-destructive thoughts
  ○ Less chronic pain
  ○ Increased resilience
  ○ Faster recovery
  ○ Long-lasting effects
- To get the most out of your loving kindness practice, incorporate it into your routine on a regular basis, either daily, weekly, or monthly.
- Always send loving kindness to yourself first. If you can only do a short meditation, then just send loving kindness to yourself and don't worry about anyone else.
- Choose positive affirmations to use with your meditation. These should be in the present tense, starting with the words "May I…"

- Start small and gradually build up the amount of time you spend in this meditation.
- As you say the blessings, consider the meaning of the words and try to embody the feelings they evoke.
- Journal your experiences immediately after your meditation.
- Adapt the script to suit your personal circumstances. You can change the affirmations according to your needs.
- Start by sending loving kindness to yourself, then someone you love, then an acquaintance, a stranger, and someone you have problems with. Work with people in that order and if you find it a little too overwhelming, cut back the number of people you include.

CHAPTER SEVEN:

CHANTING AND MANTRA MEDITATION

"The most beautiful thing we can experience is the mysterious;
it is the source of all true art and science."
—Albert Einstein

'Mantra' is a Sanskrit term, coming from the words 'man', meaning 'mind,' and 'tra' meaning 'release.' Thus, a mantra is simply a mechanism that helps you release your mind.

A mantra is a sound, word, or phrase you repeat over and over during your meditation. Many people who struggle with breath meditations or loving kindness find that they really get on with mantra meditations. What's more, this type of meditation comes with the same wonderful array of benefits you get with other forms of meditating, including:

- Increased self-awareness
- Enhanced concentration
- Lower stress levels

- More feelings of calm
- A greater sense of self-compassion
- Feeling more positive in general

While meditation is simple, that doesn't mean it's easy. Many people struggle to maintain their focus at first. Mantra meditation is one form of meditation that helps many people enhance their focus so they can work with other types of meditation. In keeping your attention on a repeated mantra, whether silently in your mind or chanting it out loud, you help keep your awareness on the mantra with fewer intrusive thoughts.

Using mantras to achieve your goals

People come to meditation for a plethora of reasons. Your motivations will be different to mine and that's okay. Understanding your motives can help you choose the most effective mantra for your circumstances.

Some people want to experience deep states of meditation. Many meditators believe that the vibrations and sound of chanting certain syllables, such as Om, can make it easier for you to achieve this state, allowing you to feel completely at peace and releasing any blockages that have been holding you back.

You might want to work with a word or phrase that supports your reasons for meditation. For example, if you are trying to feel calmer and more content, you could try using the word 'shanti' as a mantra, which is Sanskrit for 'peace.' Or, if you want to lift your mood, you could simply work with a word you love the sound of or that evokes feelings of happiness.

If you are looking to change the way you think, you could use positive affirmations as your mantra. Affirmations are positive statements written in the present tense and first person, which can speak directly to your subconscious to give you a different perspective on life. The options here are limitless, but to give you an idea of the kind of thing you might like to use, you could say, *I am happy, healthy, and wealthy,* or *I am filled with peace and love for myself and others.* If you're struggling to break out of negative thought cycles or patterns of behaviour, you could use something simple like *Let it go.*

As always, journaling can help you track your progress and observe the impact of your mantra practice.

Scientific evidence supporting mantra meditation

Transcendental meditation (TM) is a form of mantra meditation. Thanks to organizations dedicated to the study of TM, there is a wealth of evidence demonstrating it has a positive effect. It has been shown to improve physical problems such as high blood pressure, heart disease and addiction, as well as mental health conditions like stress, anxiety, depression, and PTSD.

There is also research into other types of mantra meditation, such as a 2012 study into Kriya Kirtan meditation. This 11-minute meditation involves chanting "Sa Ta Na Ma" while repeating specific hand gestures. Participants in the study experienced improved cerebral blood flow and cognitive function, which resulted in greater positive feelings, less anxiety and fatigue, and enhanced memory.

Research carried out in 2017 discovered that certain mantras could be responsible for the changes because chanting helps to synchronize the left and right hemispheres of the brain, as well as produce more alpha brainwaves. Over time, it is possible this synchronization could improve brain function and delay age-related cognitive decline.

Finding your mantra

There really is no right or wrong when it comes to picking a mantra. Your options are literally limitless! However, for some people, having so much choice can be daunting, so here are a few things to consider when you choose a mantra:

- You can work with a single syllable or sound, such as Om. Many people believe that Om contains the original sound of the universe and it has been chanted by so many people all over the world that it contains a massive amount of power to connect to. Working with an abstract sound like this means you won't be distracted by pondering the meaning of the word or phrase.
- Other popular mantras include 'So Hum' (I am), 'Om Mani Padme Hum' (the jewel is in the lotus), or 'Aham Brahmasmi' (I am divine).
- You can use mantras to clear your chakras of any blocks. Chakras are energy centres in the etheric body that control the flow of energy throughout the body. Some believe that if any of the chakras are blocked, this can give rise to mental, physical, or emotional problems. The mantras for the chakras are:
  - Lam – the root chakra
  - Vam – the sacral chakra
  - Ram – the solar plexus chakra
  - Yam – the heart chakra
  - Ham – the throat chakra
  - Om or Aum – the third eye chakra
  - Om or Ah – the crown chakra
- Some people are uncomfortable using a sound or phrase they don't understand and prefer working with something more

familiar. As previously mentioned, you could also chant a word or phrase that embodies your goals or aspirations. If you decide to take this approach, choose something positive. You might find yourself gaining new insights as you chant your phrase or simply feeling in more alignment with your mantra. It's entirely up to you how long or short your mantra is. You could say "I am filled with peace" or simply chant the word "peace," depending on what works for you. It's all about finding your personal preference and going with it.

How to meditate with a mantra

Go somewhere quiet where you can meditate without being interrupted. Make yourself comfortable, whether that's sitting in a chair or on the floor or lying down.

Set a timer for however long you want to meditate. As always, start with just a few minutes and gradually increase the time.

Take a moment to connect with your breath without trying to control or change it in any way. Simply focus on the feeling of the breath flowing in and out of your body.

When you're ready, start silently chanting your mantra in your mind. You will probably find that your mantra will naturally begin to follow your breath. Let your mantra flow at whatever speed it will – if you're working with a phrase, you'll probably want to say it with the inhale and repeat it with the exhale; if you're working with a word or sound, you might want to repeat it multiple times per breath or stretch it out to match the length of your breath. As always, feel free to experiment to find what works for you.

If you notice your thoughts starting to wander, gently acknowledge the disturbance, let the thought drift away, and bring your attention back to your mantra.

When your timer goes off, take a moment to sit with yourself as you let your mantra die off. You might like to take a few deep inhalations and exhalations before coming out of your meditation. Remember to journal your experiences to note the impact of your mantra.

Using mala beads

Some people find mala beads helpful when working with a mantra. These are a form of prayer beads, a little like a Catholic rosary. Traditionally, they have 108 beads, as well as what's called a 'guru bead,' which is larger than the others and usually has a tassel.

Mala beads help you stay focused during a mantra meditation because the repetitive movement of your fingers with the beads helps you stay grounded, while touching each bead enables you to keep track of how many times you've repeated your mantra. When you use mala beads, you can dispense with a timer because your beads will tell you when you've finished your meditation.

To use mala beads with a mantra:

- Hold the beads in one hand.
- Let it fall across your fingers so you can easily move it. Put two fingers around a bead next to the guru bead. You might like to use your thumb and middle finger to reflect the fact that some religious traditions won't use the index finger.
- Say your mantra as you inhale and exhale for one full breath.
- Move your fingers to the next bead, repeating your mantra with another inhalation and exhalation.
- Keep doing this with each bead until you've made your way around the chain and are back at the guru bead.
- If you would like to do a longer meditation, go round the chain another time until you return to the guru bead.

Changing your mantra

You can change your mantra at any time. If you find you're not resonating with your first choice, try a different mantra. You might want to meditate with the same mantra for a month to deepen your understanding or connection with it, but if you're really struggling with a mantra, there's nothing wrong with changing it for something that speaks to you more.

You could also use different mantras for different occasions. You might decide you want to meditate first thing in the morning and last thing at night, so you could use a mantra in the morning to make you treat everyone you meet with compassion. In the evening you might want to relax and calm down, so you use a different mantra to reflect that feeling. There are no rules other than to do what works for you.

Chanting

Put simply, chanting is repeating your mantra out loud. So, just as before, you can chant a sound, word, or phrase, simply repeating it aloud over and over. If you are using a single word, such as 'yes,' 'peace,' or 'calm,' you might like to say it once with the exhalation, pausing when you inhale. Alternatively, you could repeat it multiple times with each exhalation. Go with what feels most comfortable.

If you're using a phrase, try to time it so it coincides with a single exhalation.

Experiment with volume levels. You could say it at a normal volume, fill the room with your breath and make it louder, or whisper it. How do the different levels make you feel? You may find that one particular approach makes it easier for you to enter a meditative trance than others.

How to chant 'Om'

Chanting the sound 'Om' can be one of the most invigorating, profound practices. It can be practiced on its own for a set amount of time or you might like to end your meditation with a single intonation, even if you've been working with a completely different technique.

Make yourself comfortable, sitting upright so the breath can flow freely as you intone. You might like to sit cross legged with your hands lightly resting on your knees, palms facing up as your thumb and index finger touch.

Close your eyes and inhale deeply. Exhale slowly, allowing your body to relax.

Inhale deeply again and with your next inhalation, chant the sound 'Om.' Let your breath make the sound rather than chanting from your throat. Let it flow freely from your belly, in a sound half-way between singing and speaking.

When you feel your breath coming to an end, let the Om finish naturally before you run out of air. Inhale deeply and intone Om with your exhalation. Repeat for as long as you like.

The most important aspect of this process is to feel the vibration in your body rather than trying to be as loud or go as long as possible. Observe yourself as you chant, feeling the energy starting at the bottom of your body with the 'O' sound and rising through your body so the 'mm' sound fills your head.

Don't be afraid to subtly adjust your jaw or head position to allow for an easier flow of breath. You should aim to make a clean sound with no catches or rasps. You might find it helpful if you imagine you're sending the sound to the end of the universe, reaching out far and wide in all directions.

Chapter Summary

- Mantra meditations are as effective as other forms of meditation in supporting your physical, mental, and emotional wellbeing.
- Benefits include:
  - Increased self-awareness
  - Enhanced concentration
  - Lower stress levels
  - More feelings of calm
  - A greater sense of self-compassion
  - Feeling more positive in general
- You can use mantras to help you reach your goals. Choose a mantra that supports what you are looking to achieve, e.g., using the word 'calm' if you want to feel more peaceful and less stressed.
- There is a wealth of scientific evidence to support the positive impact of mantra meditation, particularly transcendental meditation, which uses mantra.
- It is entirely up to you what mantra you work with. Choose one that resonates with you and is aligned with your aims:
  - You can work with a single syllable or sound.
  - You can work with a phrase.
  - You can work with mantras associated with the chakras.
  - You can work with a mantra in another language so you aren't distracted by the meaning of the words.
  - You can work with a mantra in a language you understand to help you connect with the meaning of the word.
- The technique for working with a mantra is very simple. You just repeat the sound, word, or phrase silently in your mind.

You will probably find that your mantras become coordinated with your breath. Go with what feels most comfortable.

- You might find it helpful to use mala beads to keep track of your mantra and support you to stay focused.
- Don't be afraid to change your mantra to suit your needs.
- Chanting involves repeating your mantra out loud.
- One popular form of chanting is to intone the sound 'Om.' Let the breath flow freely as you chant the word with your out breath. Let the Om finish before you run out of air.
- Note the way the sound vibrates in your body. You might feel it starting at the bottom of your body, rising to the top of your head as you end the sound.
- It can be helpful to imagine you're sending the sound out to the end of the universe, filling it with your chanting.

CHAPTER EIGHT:

MOVING MEDITATIONS

"Meditation is the ultimate mobile device; you can use it anywhere, anytime, unobtrusively."
—Sharon Salzberg

Most people think of meditation as being a sedentary activity. This is why some people really struggle with meditation and think they can't do it. Sitting still is incredibly difficult for some people and it's impossible to calm and focus the mind if all you can think about is how you need to fight the urge to fidget.

However, if this is you, don't worry. I've got you covered! You might enjoy doing a movement meditation. This involves shifting your consciousness while moving your body. The most widespread example of a moving meditation is yoga, which brings together a meditative state with gentle movements of the body. Other examples include qigong, tai chi, and aikido. Dance can even be treated as a form of meditation in the right circumstances.

It is outside the scope of this book to dig into these more formal types of movement meditation, but if you think you might like to learn more about them, I suggest you look into local classes to study with a qualified instructor.

Moving meditation is a way of engaging the body so you can calm the mind and be fully present in the moment. In fact, for some people, movement meditation can be far more effective at stilling inner chatter than other more traditional stationary meditations. If you're someone you enjoys extreme sports, you may find that the easiest way for you to enter a meditative state is while you're doing a challenging physical activity that demands your total attention.

The benefits of movement meditation

A movement meditation confers the same kinds of benefits as other types of meditation, such as lowering blood pressure and stress levels. However, moving your body also brings with it a number of other benefits. For example, a session of chakra dance meditation has been estimated to burn as many as 600 calories, making it a workout for body *and* mind. Moving your body can also help you feel more centred and grounded, connecting you to the world around you, making you more mindful and in the moment.

What's more, research has shown that moving can improve your cognitive function, learning, and memory. In one study, it was found that students who made specific physical gestures that were linked to vocabulary words found it easier to recall them. Another positive side effect is that movement can reinforce the development of new habits, although you should be aware that this is true of both good *and* bad habits, so be mindful about what you're doing when you move.

Getting started with movement meditation

Your movements don't need to be large or exaggerated. This is a very simple movement meditation that can help you decide whether this is the right form of meditation for you.

- Ideally, start your meditation from a standing position, although you can sit if this is uncomfortable for you. Keep your legs relaxed, knees in a soft bend.
- Turn your attention to your feet and how they feel against the ground. You might like to wiggle your toes and observe the sensation. Are you wearing socks or shoes, or are you barefoot? How does that feel? What are the textures beneath your feet?
- Draw your focus up your body. If you're sitting down, observe how your body is connected to your seat and where you feel any pressure against your body. If you're standing, become aware of the space all around you.
- Now bring your attention to your breath. As you inhale, allow your arms to rise. As you exhale, let them lower. Continue this gentle movement, letting the arms move with the flow of your breath for the length of your meditation.
- After you've finished, you should journal about your experiences. You may well find that you experienced fewer intrusive thoughts because moving makes it harder for those thoughts to come through while you're focused on moving your body.

Slow hands moving meditation

- Make yourself comfortable, either sitting cross-legged on the floor or upright on a chair.

- Let your hands rest gently on your thighs as you bring your awareness to your breath and then down to your hands.
- As you enter into a meditative state, feel energy flowing into your hands.
- When you feel ready, gradually lift your hands up, paying close attention to the sensation of movement.
- Slowly raise your hands in front of you and then turn the palms to face each other.
- Spend a moment observing the flow of energy between your hands.
- When you are ready, allow your hands to slowly return back to your thighs.

Walking meditations

Walking meditations can be difficult to get into, but once you master them, they can be one of the most engaging forms of meditation. There are a lot of variations on walking meditations, so pick one that appeals to you and start with that before going on to explore other techniques.

1. As you walk, pay close attention to your feet. Observe the sensation of your feet touching the ground and then lifting again. Be aware of the world around you. Look for things you've never noticed before. Look at the trees and see how they move in the breeze. Think about how many colours you can identify. Be fully present as you walk.

2. Coordinate your breath with your footsteps. You might like to inhale for four steps and exhale for four steps. As you feel yourself entering a meditative state, you might like to extend your breath. Can you inhale and exhale for eight steps? Twelve steps?

3. Let the universe dictate the direction of your walk. This is a good meditation to do if you're walking around a town or city. Whenever you reach an intersection, look for the direction with a 'walk' sign and go that way. You are walking without a specific destination in mind. Giving up responsibility for where you walk is a good way to stay in the present moment. Observe how you're feeling as you get farther and farther away from where you began your walk. How is your body feeling? What thoughts come up for you?

4. Do a gratitude walk. With every step, say something you're grateful for. If this means you have to slow down while you think of something, then do so. Take as long as you need with each step.

5. A Buddhist walking meditation known as *kinhin* involves going for a slow, contemplative walk in between bouts of sitting meditation. This can be a good way to build up your ability to do sitting meditations. Do a simple sitting meditation, such as observing your breath for three minutes, then walk slowly around the room in a clockwise direction. Meditate for another three minutes then go for another slow walk. Continue to repeat this pattern for as long as you need.

Dance meditation

Dance can be a good way to lose yourself in the moment. Choose a song or piece of music that brings you joy and simply allow your body to move in whatever way feels right. Don't worry about being graceful or coordinated. The important thing is to let your body do whatever it wants, regardless of how it looks.

Chapter Summary

- People who struggle to stay still long enough to meditate might find it easier to do a moving meditation.
- Common examples of moving meditations include yoga, qigong, tai chi, aikido, and dance.
- Moving meditations combine all the benefits of more traditional forms of meditation, along with the advantages of gentle movement. Studies have shown they can improve your cognitive function, learning, and memory, and can also help you to develop new habits.
- A simple moving meditation is to raise and lower your arms in harmony with your breath.
- A slow hands moving meditation is a similar meditation, but with this, you start with your hands on your thighs. Let them slowly rise, turning the palms to face each other. Stay here for a while, noticing the flow of energy between your hands before letting them gently fall back to your thighs.
- There are a number of different variations of walking meditations:
    - As you walk, keep your focus on your feet. Spend some time being fully aware of the sensations your feet are experiencing as you move. Then turn your focus to the world around you, observing every little detail.
    - Coordinate your breath with your steps. Try inhaling for four steps then exhaling for four.
    - Let the universe decide where you're going to walk. Every time you reach an intersection, go in the direction of the 'walk' sign.
    - Do a gratitude walk and list something you're grateful for with every step.

- ○ Alternate doing a walking meditation with a sitting meditation. Spend a few minutes doing a meditation sitting down then slowly walk around the room in a clockwise direction. Keep switching between the two for as long as you want.
- Dance your way into meditation. Put on some music that makes you want to dance and let your body move however it wants.

CHAPTER NINE:

GUIDED VISUALIZATION

"The mind is definitely something that can be transformed, and meditation is a means to transform it."

—Dalai Lama

Guided visualizations are one of the most popular types of meditation. There are countless videos on YouTube that will take you through beautiful meditations for anything you can imagine, from relieving stress, manifesting money, or balancing your chakras to attracting love, trusting more, or finding your life's purpose.

The beauty of guided visualizations is that they do a lot of the heavy lifting for you. All you have to do is make yourself comfortable and follow along with the instructions. For many people, this is one of the most accessible forms of meditation.

However, there is a small subset of people for whom this is the most challenging way to meditate. Approximately 10% of the population cannot see things in their mind's eye. If you've always struggled to visualize things, then it's likely you fall into this minority. There's nothing wrong with you. It's just the way your brain is wired. But it's worth being aware of this because if you've tried guided visualizations in the past and found them difficult, you may have thought you were doing something wrong. You weren't. It's just something which doesn't work for you.

If you are one of the 10%, it's unlikely you'll ever be able to visualize to the extent that you can see the images you are being guided to create in your mind. However, this doesn't mean you can't follow along. After all, you can't see the back of your head, but you know it's there because you can feel and sense it. When you get up in the night to fetch yourself a drink of water, you can't see the room around you because it's dark, but you still know where everything is because you're familiar with your surroundings.

It's the same with guided visualizations. Let's say you were asked to imagine yourself on a beach. Don't force yourself to try and see the ocean. Instead, think about the sounds around you, the cawing of the seagulls, and the crash of the waves against the shoreline. Feel the spray of salt water against your skin. Feel the warmth of the sun shining down on you. Immerse yourself in the emotions of feeling safe and relaxed on a day out. Simply *know* that the ocean is in front of you and don't worry about whether you can see it or not.

Working from a script

In the rest of this chapter, you'll find a number of guided visualization scripts. You can try to memorize them before you go into your meditation, but you'll find it much easier if you record them for yourself or get someone else to read them to you if you don't like the sound of your own voice. You can always partner up with someone so that they read a script for you and then you do the same for them.

When the script is being read to you rather than you attempting to remember what's supposed to happen, it's much easier to immerse yourself in the experience. If your brain is engaged in retrieving things from memory, it'll be very difficult to enter into a meditative state.

Feel free to adapt these scripts for your personal use. It might be that you need to make a few adjustments to them to suit a specific purpose, so treat these as a source of inspiration rather than being set in stone. You also may like the look of a meditation but have a problem with some aspects of it. For example, you might enjoy sitting by the ocean but don't like the feel of sand beneath your feet, so you could take out any reference to walking barefoot on the sand. Remember – this is your meditation experience, so do whatever you need to make it as enjoyable and easy for yourself as possible.

When you've finished your meditation, journal your experiences. Some guided visualizations are designed for you to receive messages or answers to questions you may have. Sometimes the full significance of them isn't immediately clear and it's only when you later reflect on them that you understand what you were given. I often find that this gives me even further confirmation that my meditations are working and helping me to lead a richer, fuller life.

Meditation to release any worries

This meditation takes you to a safe place where you can freely talk about anything that is bothering you and release it so you don't have to worry about it anymore.

Make yourself comfortable, either sitting upright or lying down, and close your eyes.

Turn your attention to your breath. Let it flow as it will without trying to control or change it in anyway.

And as you observe the flow of breath in…and out…in…and out…you notice that the sound of your breath becomes the sound of a light breeze blowing around you.

You realize you are sitting somewhere high. Maybe you are up on a gentle slope, just high enough for you to see the world around you, or maybe you are on the top of a tall mountain, practically touching the sky.

Wherever you are, you are comfortable, and you are safe and secure. This is a place of peace. There is nothing here that can hurt you.

Take a moment to gaze around and enjoy the view. It's breath-taking and you can see for miles around. You hear the sound of eagles cawing as they swoop and soar around you. You feel the light kiss of the wind against your skin. The air feels lighter here, reflecting the altitude.

This is your time to rest and relax, letting go of anything worrying you.

You lie back on the slope and watch the clouds floating across the sky. As they gently wend their way across the sky, they slowly twist into interesting shapes and patterns, and you spend a while trying to spot pictures in the clouds.

As you lie here, you realize your breath is forming little clouds that lightly float up to join the other clouds in the sky. You now have the chance to let your breath carry away your stresses and worries.

In your mind, start talking about the things you want to release or let go. You might like to talk about your worries and fears. You might like to talk about people who are upsetting you. You might like to talk about the people or situations causing you stress. Or you can simply say, *I am letting go of anything that no longer serves me.*

As you speak, you can see your words gently floating away, floating up to join the other clouds in the sky where they gradually dissipate into the air.

Take as long as you need to speak about your worries and when you are done, you feel calm, relaxed, and at peace.

You can come back to this place any time you need. This is your sanctuary. But for you, it's time for you to return to your normal self.

Gently bring your focus back to your breath, feeling it come back to normal.

Start paying attention to the sounds of the room around you, feeling yourself grounding back into your body.

You might like to stretch or yawn, allowing yourself to fully return from your meditation.

When you're ready, open your eyes.

A beach visualization for deep relaxation

Sometimes you just need to experience pure relaxation to give yourself a break from the pressures of everyday life. This meditation will take you through a deep body relaxation before letting you spend some time relaxing on the beach. By the end of it, you'll be feeling incredibly relaxed and refreshed, capable of coping with anything.

Go somewhere you won't be disturbed and make yourself comfortable, either sitting or lying down.

Turn your attention to your feet and allow them to relax. Say to yourself, *feet relax.*

Bring your attention up to your shins and calves and allow them to relax. Say to yourself, *shins and calves relax.*

Bring your attention up to your knees and allow them to relax. Say to yourself, *knees relax.*

Bring your attention up to your thighs and allow them to relax. Say to yourself, *thighs relax.*

Now observe your legs, noticing how they're more relaxed than when you started. Can they relax even further? Say to yourself, *legs relax.*

Now bring your attention up to your lower abdomen and back and allow them to relax. Say to yourself, *lower and abdomen and back relax.*

Bring your attention up to your belly and allow it to relax. Say to yourself, *belly relax.*

Bring your attention up to your chest and allow it to relax, letting your breath flow freely and easily. Say to yourself, *chest relax.*

Now observe your torso, noticing how it's more relaxed than when you started. Can it relax even further? Say to yourself, *torso relax.*

Now bring your attention to your shoulders and allow them to relax. Say to yourself, *shoulders relax.*

Bring your attention down your arms and allow them to relax. Say to yourself, *arms relax.*

Bring your attention to your wrists and hands and allow them to relax. Say to yourself, *wrists and arms relax.*

Now observe all of your arms, noticing how they're more relaxed than when you started.

Can they relax even further? Say to yourself, *arms relax.*

Now bring your attention to your neck and allow it to soften and relax. Say to yourself, *neck relax.*

Bring your attention to your face and allow it to soften and relax, smoothing away any worry line. Say to yourself, *face relax.*

Bring your attention to the top of your head and allow it to relax. Say to yourself, *head relax.*

Now observe all of your head, your neck, your face, your ears, the crown of your head. Notice it's more relaxed than when you started. Can it relax even further? Say to yourself, *head relax.*

Now lightly scan your whole body from your head to your toes. Feel how you are so wonderfully relaxed. Can you become even more relaxed? Say to yourself, *body relax.*

Now inhale deeply, pulling the air into your diaphragm, filling your lungs...and exhale slowly, letting go of any last lingering traces of stress or tension.

And as you keep your focus on your breath, you start to hear the sound of the ocean, gently caressing the shoreline. It is a beautifully sunny day, the sun warm on your face as you realize you're walking through a tropical forest towards the sound of the sea.

As you make your way towards the ocean, the sound of the waves gets louder and louder. You can smell the ocean spray in the air, practically tasting the salt in your mouth. You hear the sound of seagulls circling overhead, lazily enjoying the sunshine.

Up ahead, you see the brilliant blue colour of the pure ocean water. You could cut through the trees and find yourself walking along a beautiful stretch of soft white sand. You take off your shoes and take a moment to stand still, luxuriating in the feeling of the sand between your toes. Scrunch your toes and feel the sand moving beneath your feet.

When you are ready, start walking towards the water again. You come to a stop at the point where the waves meet the sand and watch the waves flowing up…and down…up…and down…

Gradually, they come closer and closer to you until a wave washes over your feet, lightly touching your toes.

You enjoy the sensation of the warm, tropical water moving across your feet and you might decide to walk further into the water. You may even like to go for a swim. No one is here. You are completely alone, private, and safe. You can go into the water and swim around without worrying about anyone finding you.

The sun is so warm and the water temperature is perfect. Whether you choose to swim, immerse yourself in the water, paddle, or simply sit on the sand and watch the movement of the waves, this is a moment of complete peace and tranquillity.

When you are ready, come out of the water and continue to walk along the strand. Up ahead you see an empty lounge chair with a towel folded on top of it. You realize that this chair has been placed here for you. You can relax on the chair or you can spread the towel on the sand and lie back to soak in the sun.

You feel more relaxed than you ever have before. Any stress or tension is long since gone. You can spend as long as you like enjoying this feeling of deep relaxation.

When you're ready, you can leave the beach, but you can come back here anytime you need. This is your place, and it is always here waiting for you.

Turn your attention back to your breath. Notice how it's changed since you started this meditation.

Inhale deeply, hold it for a moment, then release.

Stretch and yawn, feeling yourself becoming more alert, returning to your usual state of being.

When you're ready, open your eyes.

Candle visualization for relaxation

This is a different approach to helping you be more relaxed and in the moment. You will visualize a candle and simply observe it from a number of angles. This will help pull you into the present moment to be more mindful.

Find somewhere you won't be disturbed and make yourself comfortable.

Close your eyes and turn your attention to your breath.

Inhale deeply, hold it for a moment, then exhale fully.

With your next inhalation, feel yourself breathing in a beautiful, healing energy.

Hold it for a moment, and as you exhale, breathe out any stress or tension.

Breathe in healing.

Breathe out tension.

Breathe in healing.

Breathe out tension.

Stay here for a while, just enjoying this sensation of relaxing more and more with every breath.

Gradually, you realize that you are in a room. The room is dark, but you feel safe and secure here. There is nothing that can harm you and you feel comfortable and relaxed.

You become aware that there is a candle next to you, sending out a gentle glow into the room. Its flames flicker and dance, sending fascinating patterns of light and shadow across the room.

Sit here for a moment as you watch the patterns cast on the wall in front of you. The movement of the candle flame is mesmerizing, and it helps you to relax even more.

When you're ready, turn your attention to look at the candle. Turn your attention to its flame.

What colour is the flame? Do you notice any blue around the wick? Is the flame yellow or orange? Is it large or small? How does it change as it burns?

Now focus on the candle. What colour is it? What shape? Is it large or small? Has it been burning for long or is it newly lit? Observe without judgment as you build an image of the candle in front of you.

As the candle burns, the wax melts. Know that it is melting away any stress or tension you're feeling. This candle represents your fears or worries and as it slowly burns, melting the wax, it takes away a little of your stress, and then a little more, and a little more, as you relax more and more and more.

Maybe you notice some wax dripping down the side of the candle. With each drip, another source of tension goes away, and another…and another.

As the candle burns, you feel more relaxed than you ever have before.

You notice that the candle is in a holder, which makes it easy for you to pick it up.

You pick it up and hold it in front of you. Watch how the flame flickers every time you exhale, dancing in tune with your breath.

Take a few moments to watch the flame and how it responds to your breath.

When you are ready, inhale deeply and exhale sharply, blowing out the candle.

Feel yourself coming back into your body, becoming more aware of the present moment.

Stretch, yawn, and when you are ready, open your eyes.

Guided visualization to prepare you to give a presentation or speech

Go somewhere you won't be disturbed and make yourself comfortable. Sit with your back supported so you can relax but stay upright.

Turn your attention to your breath.

Take a deep breath in…and out…

And with each breath, feel yourself becoming more and more relaxed. Allow any stress or tension to melt away with each exhalation and breathe in peace and relaxation with every inhalation.

And as you continue to breathe in peace and relaxation, send that beautiful feeling of peace to any part of your body that seems tense.

Now I want you to think back to a time when you were really excited about something.

Maybe it was when you were a child, excited about Christmas. Maybe it was when you had a holiday booked and you were excited about going away. Maybe it was when you had tickets to see your favourite band and you were excited about seeing them play.

Feel the sensation of being happy and excited as you allow yourself to think about public speaking.

And as you allow the subject of public speaking to come to mind, notice your reaction to it. Do you feel anything in your body? What emotions come up for you?

Maybe public speaking has been a source of stress or anxiety for you in the past, but now you know that it's possible to be calm and relaxed when you think about giving a presentation or speech.

You can be at peace and relaxed.

You can be calm and relaxed.

Those feelings of stress or anxiety can become feelings of excitement.

Let that excitement fill you with energy. You have the opportunity to help people with your speech. Let that thought make you feel excited. You look forward to the chance to give a public speech.

Remember that feeling of excitement you had earlier and now bring that feeling to the idea of public speaking. Spend a moment really embodying that feeling and then let it gently flow away as you bring yourself back to pure relaxation.

Focus on your breath once more, breathing in peace and relaxation with every inhalation. Breathe out tension, fear, anxiety, or nervousness with every exhalation. Feel yourself becoming more and more relaxed, knowing you can enjoy this feeling any time you like.

Now I want you to know that you can give successful talks anytime you like. You can enjoy this experience, knowing that people are enjoying your speech, listening carefully to what you have to say.

Picture yourself as being a confident, accomplished speaker. What would that feel like for you? How would it feel to know that you're filled with confidence, fully in control of the situation, capable of talking about your chosen subject with knowledge and eloquence?

In your mind's eye, see yourself getting ready to give a speech. As you put together your notes for your talk, feel how excited you are, how happy you are that you've been invited to give this speech.

When the time comes for you to speak, feel how confident you are knowing that you are fully prepared and will be giving an amazing presentation.

See yourself going to the venue of your talk. Feel how excited you are. You can't wait to give this talk! You know exactly what you want to say and you know how much people are going to love what you're about to say.

See yourself walking into the place where you're going to give your talk. Maybe it's a theatre, lecture room, auditorium, meeting room. Wherever it is, it is packed with people who are eagerly waiting for your talk. It makes you even more excited and happy to see just how many people are here, desperate to see you.

Now walk to the front of the room. It is time for you to give your presentation. The room falls quiet as everyone waits to hear what you've got to say.

Look out at the crowd waiting for you to speak. You might like to look down at your notes to refresh your memory before you begin your talk, but there's no need. You already know every word of what you're about to say and you really don't need your notes.

You start your speech and you've never felt so confident. You are engaging and entertaining and the audience is hanging off your every word. Throughout your talk, you remain calm and focused. You are relaxed, enjoying the moment. Your ideas flow freely and all the preparation you've done has really paid off. This is the best talk you've ever given, and you feel amazing! You wish this moment could go on forever.

When you've finished your talk, the applause is deafening. People loved what you said and they wish you could speak longer. They've enjoyed the experience as much as you have.

You invite questions from the audience, and you are able to answer each one with confidence. Even if you don't know the answer, you feel secure in saying that you'll find it out and come back to them. You know that it's okay not to have all the answers and this is an opportunity for you to build a relationship with someone who needs more information.

The audience is even more impressed with how you've handled the questions.

As you leave the stage or lectern, the audience breaks into applause once again.

You are so happy with how you've performed. You feel incredible and even a little sad that your speech is over because you had so much fun.

You will remember how confident and calm you felt in this moment. You can experience this feeling at any time. You can feel like this for every speech you ever give and you can always come back to this meditation whenever you need to help you prepare for a presentation.

Take a moment to bask in this feeling of accomplishment and confidence.

When you are ready, turn your attention back to your breath. Notice how it is slow and calm, reflecting how calm you feel about public speaking.

Inhale deeply, hold it for a moment, then let it go.

And when you're ready, open your eyes.

Meditation to help you love and accept your body

This meditation will help you develop a more positive relationship with your body. Most of us are our own worst critics. Accepting your body for how it is right now will help you accept yourself unconditionally, raising your self-esteem and allowing you to feel more confident with yourself.

Go somewhere you won't be disturbed. Make yourself comfortable, either sitting or lying down.

Close your eyes and turn your attention to your breath. Observe it flowing in…and out…in…and out…

And with every inhalation, feel your body becoming more and more relaxed.

And with every exhalation, breathe out anything that is bothering you, any worries or stresses you need to let go.

As you feel yourself relaxing, notice your whole body becoming warm and relaxed. As your body relaxes, feel your mind also relaxing, letting go of any tension or anxiety.

You feel calm. You feel relaxed. You feel at peace. You are completely in the moment.

I want you now to think about your body. Observe without judgment any feelings that brings up for you. Give those feelings a name and then let them go. These thoughts are temporary, and you can change how you think at any time.

Think about how you would like to feel about your body. Think about how it would feel to accept how you look right now without criticism or judgment.

Your body is an incredible machine. Whatever its shape and size, your body is performing miracles every single day. Your body carries you through this life and allows you to experience the world around you.

Turn your attention to your feet. Think about your toes. Maybe they're small and crooked, maybe they're big and straight, maybe they're a mix. However they look, each and every one is perfect just as it is.

Think about your feet. Maybe they're big. Maybe they're small. Maybe they're straight. Maybe they're crooked. Maybe they're different sizes. Maybe they match.

Your toes and feet support you to move and get to wherever you want to go. Take a moment to say thank you to your feet for supporting you.

Now consider your legs. Your legs are amazing. Maybe they're long and maybe they're short. Maybe they're thick or maybe they're skinny. Maybe they have freckles or marks. Maybe they're hairy.

Whatever your legs look like, they are incredible. They help you move around and take you to where you want to go. Take a moment to say thank you to your legs for supporting you.

Now consider your belly. Your belly is an important part of your body. Maybe your belly is big or maybe it's small. Maybe it's toned or maybe it's rounded. Whatever the case, your belly supports the systems that help to process the food you eat to give you the fuel you need to get everything done. Take a moment to say thank you to your belly for helping to feed you.

Now bring your attention up to your chest. Your chest holds your lungs and heart. Without these, you wouldn't be alive – that's incredible! Maybe your chest is toned or maybe it's not. Maybe it has freckles and moles or maybe it's smooth and clear.

Whatever your chest looks like, it's beautiful. Say thank you to your chest for keeping your heart and lungs safe.

Now bring your attention up to your back and shoulders. They're an important part of your body. They help you lift things and carry them around. They support you to stand up straight. However they look, they serve a crucial function.

Say thank you to your back and shoulders for helping you carry things around and holding you up straight.

Now bring your attention to your arms and hands. How lucky you are to have arms and hands! Maybe they're long or maybe they're short. Maybe they're elegant or maybe they're clumsy. Whatever they look like, your arms and hands let you hug the people you love. They let you give people gifts and do things to help others. They can offer comfort to someone when they're feeling sad and give someone a high five when they've got something to celebrate.

Say thank you to your arms and hands for all the things they do for you every day.

Now bring your attention up to your face, your beautiful, wonderful face. No one else has a face exactly like yours. Whatever you look like, your smile lights up other people's lives. Your face expresses your inner thoughts and helps you to connect with the people around you.

Your face is amazing. Say thank you to your face for helping you to express yourself.

Remember that however you look, you are perfectly you!

As we grow and age, our bodies will always change, but one thing will remain the same – your body will always be beautiful and special in its own right.

Take a moment to send love to every cell in your body. Feel grateful for how your body has supported you over the years and give thanks for all the experiences your body has made possible.

Your body will always be with you. Say thank you to it one more time as it takes you through this world and takes you on new and exciting adventures every single day.

Start to feel even more connected to your body as you start to return to normality. Wriggle your fingers, wriggle your toes. Stretch and yawn.

When you are ready, open your eyes.

Guided meditation for positivity

If you find it difficult to have a positive mindset, this meditation will help you reprogram your thoughts, letting go of anything troubling you and replacing negativity with a more positive attitude.

Go somewhere you won't be disturbed and make yourself comfortable, either sitting or standing down.

Turn your attention to your breath and take a moment to connect with it.

Inhale for a count of four, hold it for two, then exhale for a count of four and pause for a count of two.

Inhale for a count of four, hold it for two, then exhale for a count of four and pause for a count of two.

Inhale for a count of four, hold it for two, then exhale for a count of four and pause for a count of two.

Now inhale deeply and then exhale completely, sending out any stress or tension.

You feel much lighter as you let your breathing flow however it wants.

You realize you are sitting by a river. The sun is shining, the birds are singing, and you feel safe, peaceful and calm.

In this place, you can let every worry, every problem, every negative thought float away with the water of the river.

Pluck a blade of grass from the ground and whisper into it something that is bothering you. Toss the grass into the river and watch it float away, taking that concern with it.

Pick another blade of grass and tell it something else that is stressing you. Throw that blade of grass in the river and let it float away, taking away the stress.

Spend as long as you like giving every negative thought, every doubt, every fear, every worry to the river. Let them all float away, leaving your mind clear and refreshed.

As you sit by the river, you hear a voice whispering into your ear. It tells you, *In this moment, I am happy. In this moment, I am worthy. In this moment, I have everything I need.*

This voice continues to repeat the phrases and you find yourself joining in with them.

In this moment, I am happy. In this moment, I am worthy. In this moment, I have everything I need. in this moment, I am happy. In this moment, I am worthy. In this moment, I have everything I need.

As you repeat the phrases over and over, you feel your mind settling and calming even further, the waters of the river becoming clear and crisp.

In this moment, I am happy. In this moment, I am worthy. In this moment, I have everything I need. in this moment, I am happy. In this moment, I am worthy. In this moment, I have everything I need.

You realize that the voice you heard is your own voice. This is how you feel about yourself right now.

In this moment, I am happy. In this moment, I am worthy. In this moment, I have everything I need. in this moment, I am happy. In this moment, I am worthy. In this moment, I have everything I need.

Take as long as you want to relax by the river. This is a safe haven for you, somewhere you can feel comfortable and at peace, free from any concerns.

When you are ready, turn your attention back to your breath. Notice how it's changed from when you started the meditation, becoming more relaxed and easier.

Inhale deeply one last time. Exhale completely and as the last of the breath leaves your lungs, you may open your eyes, feeling refreshed and ready to get on with your day.

Guided meditation to get better sleep

If you struggle to get to sleep, meditation can help you relax, increasing your chances of being able to drift off. The more you think about how you can't get to sleep, the harder it is to enter into that state. With this meditation, you'll be guided to let go of any worry around sleep, making it easier for you to drift off. What's more, this meditation will relax and refresh you, so even if you don't get much sleep, you're still going to be able to feel rejuvenated and energized rather than fatigued and drained.

Make yourself comfortable, lying down where you want to go to sleep.

Bring your attention to your breath. How are you breathing? Is your breath deep and slow, or is it fast and shallow? Observe it without judgment, accepting it as it is.

Whether your breathing is fast or slow, know that every breath is taking you closer to sleep. As you continue to monitor your breathing, feel yourself becoming more and more relaxed.

Your eyelids start to feel heavier and heavier. When you feel ready, close your eyes. It feels so good to close your heavy, tired eyes after another long day.

With your eyes closed, continue to focus on your breath. As you inhale, breathe in a calming, healing white light.

Send that breath down to your toes and as you send that healing energy, in your mind say, *toes, it's time to relax.*

Exhale and inhale more calming, healing white light. Send that breath down to your feet and as you send that healing energy, in your mind say, *feet, it's time to relax.*

Exhale and inhale more calming, healing white light. Send that breath down to your ankles and as you send that healing energy, in your mind say, *ankles, it's time to relax.*

Exhale and inhale more calming, healing white light. Send that breath down to your legs and as you send that healing energy, in your mind say, *legs, it's time to relax.*

Exhale and inhale more calming, healing white light. Send that breath down your back and as you send that healing energy, in your mind say, *back, it's time to relax.*

Exhale and inhale more calming, healing white light. Send that breath down to your belly and as you send that healing energy, in your mind say, b*elly, it's time to relax.*

Exhale and inhale more calming, healing white light. Send that breath down to your chest and as you send that healing energy, in your mind say, *chest, it's time to relax.*

Exhale and inhale more calming, healing white light. Send that breath down to your shoulders and as you send that healing energy, in your mind say, *shoulders, it's time to relax.*

Exhale and inhale more calming, healing white light. Send that breath down to your arms and as you send that healing energy, in your mind say, *arms, it's time to relax.*

Exhale and inhale more calming, healing white light. Send that breath down to your hands and as you send that healing energy, in your mind say, *hands, it's time to relax.*

Exhale and inhale more calming, healing white light. Send that breath down to your neck and as you send that healing energy, in your mind say, *neck, it's time to relax.*

Exhale and inhale more calming, healing white light. Send that breath to your face and as you send that healing energy, in your mind say, *face, it's time to relax.*

Exhale and inhale more calming, healing white light. Send that breath around your whole head and as you send that healing energy, in your mind say, *head, it's time to relax.*

Exhale and inhale more calming, healing white light. Send that breath throughout your body and as you send that healing energy, in your mind say, *it's time to relax.*

Your breath is long and slow now and you feel deeply relaxed.

Continue to breathe in healing, calming energy and as you exhale, send away anything that is still causing you stress. You do not need it right now. All you need in this current moment is to focus on your breath. The pressures of your everyday life are melting away into nothing as your body slows down and prepares for sleep.

If you find your mind drifting away to relive difficult events from the day or think about everything you've got to do tomorrow, thank your mind for drawing that thought to your attention and tell it you will deal with it later. Now it's time to sleep.

Every breath takes you even closer to sleep.

And now it's time to end this meditation, but you know that even though the meditation is over, each breath will still be taking you closer and closer to sleep. It won't be long before you're deep in peaceful slumber and you will enjoy a good night's sleep, waking up feel refreshed and relaxed, ready to face the day.

Guided meditation to improve your self-belief

One thing that successful people have in common is that they all believe in themselves and their vision. If you're struggling to believe that you're capable of achieving the things you want in life, this meditation will help you improve your self-belief.

Go somewhere you won't be disturbed and make yourself comfortable.

Turn your attention to your breath.

Breathe in through your nose for a count of four.

Breathe out through your mouth for a count of four.

Inhale for a count of four.

Exhale for a count of four.

Inhale for a count of four.

Exhale for a count of four.

Now stop counting your breaths and let your breathing return to its natural flow without trying to control it in any way.

And as you continue to breathe freely, feel yourself becoming more and more relaxed, letting go of any stress or tension.

And now as you inhale, feel yourself breathing in the emotions of success, confidence, and capability.

As you exhale, breathe out any self-doubt or negative thinking that may have been holding you back from achieving your goals.

Breathe in success, confidence, and capability.

Breathe away self-doubt and negativity.

Breathe in success, confidence, and capability.

Breathe away self-doubt and negativity.

Now I want you to bring to mind a goal you have. Maybe you would like to earn more money. Maybe you would like to find the love of your life. Maybe you would like to feel fitter and healthier.

Whatever your goal, imagine that you've already achieved it. See yourself experiencing a typical day in your life after you've accomplished your goal.

Where are you?

Who are you with?

What are you doing?

How does it feel to have achieved your goal?

Make this mental picture as detailed as you possibly can. Allow yourself to feel the emotions of being the person who has everything you want as you watch yourself living the life of your dreams.

And if you notice your mind wandering off, observe those thoughts without judgment. If you find yourself doubting your abilities, simply breathe in more success, confidence, and capability, and breathe away that doubt and negativity.

Sit here, enjoying the feeling of having everything you want, knowing that you are more than capable of achieving it.

And when you're ready, open your eyes, knowing that you carry that confidence with you wherever you go. You can always tap into that feeling if you need to reassure yourself.

Guided visualization to get support with your problems

This meditation will take you to a safe place where you will meet someone who can help you solve a particular problem you might be facing. You can use this meditation as often as you like, but it's best to always go into it with an open mind. Don't assume you know whom you're going to meet. Let whoever needs to come forward come and talk to you – you may be surprised by who you encounter.

Make yourself comfortable and close your eyes.

Turn your attention to your breath. Do not try to control it in any way.

As you breathe in…and out…feel yourself becoming more and more relaxed.

Continue to listen to your breath and notice that it starts to sound like the gentle lapping of waves against the shore.

You realise you are standing on a sandy beach. The sea is lightly moving in and out…in and out, the tide slowly pulling away. You feel the kiss of sea spray on your skin.

To one side, there is a campfire, the flames gently crackling and snapping. You cross over and stand by it, letting the flames warm your hands.

A gentle breeze is blowing and for a moment you close your eyes and enjoy the feel of the air against your skin.

You realise that a path has opened up, leading away from the beach and into a forest. You start walking along the path, away from the beach. The forest is calm and quiet and you feel safe and at peace.

Eventually, the path leads you to somewhere new. It may be another beach; it might be a clearing in the forest; it might be a hill or mountain you can walk up to enjoy a beautiful view; it might be a lake. Wherever you are, it is somewhere you feel happy and at home.

As you gaze around, you notice a building. This is a place that has been built just for you.

You walk over to the building and push open the door. As you walk inside, you discover a beautiful room that has been decorated just for you. The walls are painted in your favourite colours, there are cushions and soft furnishings about the place. There are ornaments and crystals about, which have been chosen with your taste and comfort in mind.

This is the perfect meditation space and it is all yours to enjoy whenever you want.

There is a cushion in the middle of the room. You go and sit down, making yourself comfortable. Take a moment to relax and enjoy this perfect place.

There is a knock at the door. You turn and see someone enter the room you want and need to see. It may be someone you know, someone from your past or present, or it could be someone you've never met, maybe a character from history, a famous person, an author of a book you love, or simply someone new.

This person is here to help and support you. You can discuss any problems with them or ask them for advice. You can simply ask them to tell you what you need to hear right now to support you.

Take a moment to have a conversation with this person.

Your conversation draws to a close and you are left with a feeling of deep calm and peace.

You can come back to this place whenever you need. This is your place. But for now, it is time to return to the present.

Turn your attention back to your breath, feeling it return to normal.

Start listening to the sounds of the room around you, feeling yourself coming back to normality.

You may like to wriggle your fingers, wriggle your toes.

When you are ready, open your eyes.

Guided meditation to take you to your own personal relaxation space

Sometimes you just need a place to escape all the stresses and strains of your everyday life. This meditation will take you to a room that you can decorate to your own personal tastes without having to compromise to suit anyone else. Sometimes the act of being in a clean, uncluttered room is more than enough to help you let go of stress and enjoy a moment of peace and tranquillity. This meditation will enable you to create your own personal relaxation room that you can return to whenever you need to take some time out for yourself.

Make yourself comfortable and close your eyes.

Turn your attention to your breath. Do not try to control it in any way.

Gradually become aware that you are sitting in a room. It is a room you haven't seen before and yet you feel very calm and relaxed here.

There is an open window in one wall and through it you can see some trees gently swaying in the breeze. You hear the sound of birdsong through the open window, which soothes and calms you.

Turn your attention to the room. Notice how clean and organised it is. The décor is very minimalist with natural wooden floors and soothing colours on the walls.

This is your space to decorate as you wish.

You might scatter some candles around the room, a few pillows or other small items to make the space more relaxing. Play with your environment until you feel it is perfect for you.

When you have finished decorating your room, make yourself comfortable and spend some time in quiet contemplation. You might like to relive a memory that makes you happy or take a few moments to think about the things you are grateful for.

The time has come for you to leave and return to your normal life, but know that you can come back here any time you need. This is your room, your meditation space and it is always here for you.

Turn your attention back to your breath. Inhale deeply, hold for a moment and release.

And when you're ready, open your eyes.

A guided meditation for mindfulness

As we've already discussed in previous chapters, mindfulness has many documented benefits. If you've been struggling with the mindfulness exercises given earlier in this book, you may find this guided meditation a helpful way to build your ability to be in the present moment.

Go somewhere you won't be disturbed and make yourself comfortable in whatever way feels right in the moment. You could stand, sit, or lie down. You could even do this meditation as you move around the room. You can use a different position every time you do this meditation. Whatever feels right for you at this time.

Support your body to feel more open and relaxed. You might like to roll your shoulders up and back. You might like to stretch your neck by gently turning your head from side to side. Make sure your spine is straight and strong without tension. Let your muscles and joints be loose and soft, ready to explore the current moment.

Observe how your body is feeling in this moment. Do not try to change or control what you notice. You don't have to change your thoughts, feelings, or sensations. This is your time to simply be aware of what's happening without judgment. How is your body feeling in this precise moment?

Take a moment to scan your body. What sensations do you feel in your legs? Arms? Torso? Head? Do you observe any areas of tightness or tension? Are you feeling particularly relaxed in any area? Notice these feelings without judgment and without trying to change or control them.

You may like to close your eyes as you continue to explore your awareness, or you can keep them open. Do whatever feels most appropriate.

You may find that you experience thoughts or emotions as you continue to notice what's present. That's okay. This is a time for you to just be without judgment.

Tune into your breath, inhaling deeply through your nose and releasing the breath through your mouth with a sighing noise. Let this breath release any tension, breathing in air to nourish and support your body, and breathing out tension to allow yourself to soften and relax further.

After a few breaths, let your breathing return to its natural flow and observe how this has changed your body. Are you feeling more relaxed? Are you more aware of any tension in your body?

Now turn your attention to whatever is supporting your body right now. Maybe you're sitting on a chair or a cushion. Perhaps you're on a bed or even the floor. Wherever you are, sink into your body and really feel grounded into whatever it is that's supporting you. Bring awareness to the connection you have to that thing. How does it feel against your body? Is there any pressure or weight?

You may find that you still get thoughts wandering into your mind and that's okay. Thoughts are a natural function of the brain and it's normal to pay attention to the past or future. One thing is always constant though: your body is always centred in the present moment. So if you find yourself drifting into conscious thought, bring your awareness back into your body and your bodily sensations.

Bring your awareness back to your breath and watch it continue to flow in and out of your body. Is it any different to earlier in your meditation? You might like to take some deeper breaths as you connect to your breathing. You might like to watch your belly rising and falling with the breath. You could put your hands on your belly and feel this gentle movement.

Let your awareness be filled with your breath and the sensation of breathing. You are fully connected to the present moment, fully embodied in what's happening right now.

Now take a moment to give thanks to yourself for giving yourself the gift of this meditation. You have just taken some time to be fully present and mindful, with all the benefits that brings to your mind and body.

Know that you can enjoy this sense of embodied awareness at any time. Whenever you need, you can connect to your body or connect with your breath to be more present and mindful.

When you are ready, open your eyes, stretch and yawn, reconnecting with your surroundings as you come out of your meditation.

Guided meditation for forgiveness

Pain is inevitable in life. People will do things to hurt us, whether accidentally or deliberately. We all make mistakes that have a negative impact on others, which can cause serious damage.

When we experience a negative situation, we often make things worse for ourselves with judgment, anger, and blame. These are perfectly natural reactions and it's only human to feel these emotional reactions. However, when they become a problem is if we're unable to let these reactions go. And so we carry them with us, compounding the original harm.

When you practice forgiveness, you can let go of the extra baggage you're carrying. It doesn't mean that the problem behaviour is okay or that you're going to put yourself in a position where it can be repeated. You can forgive someone without ever seeing them again.

But it means you let go of the hold it has over you, clearing the way for a brighter, more positive future.

For example, think about a time when a stranger did something to annoy you. Maybe they didn't hold a door open for you or maybe they cut you off in traffic. Whatever they did, it made you angry, but they went off and got on with their lives, blithely unaware of the impact they had on you. In comparison, you can't stop thinking about what's just happened, which makes it difficult for you to enjoy the fun things you had planned for that day. When you do this, the only person you're harming is yourself.

Sometimes the person you most need to forgive is yourself. We often beat ourselves up for the mistakes we've made, feeling like we should have known or done better, when we're all just human and mistakes are a part of life.

This meditation will help you cultivate forgiveness, both towards yourself and to others.

Go somewhere you will not be disturbed and make yourself comfortable.

Close your eyes and take a moment to tune in to how you're feeling.

What emotions are you feeling?

What physical sensations can you notice?

Take a moment to just check in with yourself without judgment.

Now turn your attention to your breath. Watch it flowing in... and out...in...and out...

Now think of something you judge yourself for. Maybe it was a decision you made, something you did, or a situation you created. Notice how this memory makes you feel. Maybe you feel regret, anger, sadness, or frustration. Allow that emotion to flow through you without judgment or trying to control it.

In your mind, say to yourself, *I forgive myself for making mistakes. I forgive myself for any pain I have caused to myself and others. I forgive and accept myself for being human.*

I forgive myself for making mistakes. I forgive myself for any pain I have caused to myself and others. I forgive and accept myself for being human.

I forgive myself for making mistakes. I forgive myself for any pain I have caused to myself and others. I forgive and accept myself for being human.

Sit with these phrases and see how you feel. You may find yourself crying and that's okay. Allow this moment of emotional release.

If you find it too difficult to focus on these phrases, that's okay. Just allow yourself to focus on your breath to calm yourself down. You can always come back to these phrases at any time when you feel ready.

Now think of a time when you felt that someone mistreated you. Maybe they did this deliberately or maybe they had no idea of the harm they were causing. Bring that person into your mind's eye and send them love and forgiveness. Say to yourself, *I forgive you for making mistakes. I forgive you for any pain you caused me. I forgive and accept you for being human.*

I forgive you for making mistakes. I forgive you for any pain you caused me. I forgive and accept you for being human.

I forgive you for making mistakes. I forgive you for any pain you caused me. I forgive and accept you for being human.

As you say these words, give yourself permission to release any resentment or judgment you may be feeling around the person you need to forgive. Again, if you find this too difficult right now, that's okay. You can always come back to it another time when you feel ready.

Now turn your attention to your breath and with every inhalation, breathe in compassion for yourself.

And as you exhale, send out forgiveness to everyone you need to forgive.

Breathe in compassion.

Breathe out forgiveness.

Breathe in compassion.

Breathe out forgiveness.

You may have found this meditation difficult, so I want you to take a moment to thank yourself for having the courage to do this practice. Take a moment to observe how you're feeling and then think about what you might say to a friend who is going through a similar experience. Listen to that advice and then accept it for yourself.

Journal in your diary any insights you gleaned during this meditation.

Guided meditation for dealing with grief

Grief is one of the least understood emotions we experience. In western cultures, we have a tendency to diminish the impact of grief, feeling like it's something we just need to push through, which only make things worse.

We can experience grief following any type of loss. We're all aware that we grieve the loss of a loved one, either through bereavement or the ending of a relationship. But other types of loss can include a missed opportunity, infertility, the impact of a chronic illness, or something that forces you to change your life plans without warning. You can even feel grief around a positive event. You might be getting what you've always dreamed about, but it comes with a loss of your old, familiar life, which could mean losing friends, moving home, and experiencing other major changes in. your life.

Whatever the cause of your grief, don't be afraid to seek help and support. There are many charities that give comfort to people suffering with grief due to a variety of reasons.

This meditation is another way in which you can offer kindness to yourself during this difficult time as you come to terms with your loss.

Go somewhere you won't be disturbed and make yourself comfortable.

Close your eyes and focus on your breath. Inhale deeply and ask you exhale, feeling your body sink into relaxation.

Inhale and as you exhale, feel your body relax even more.

Inhale again and as you exhale, let your body relax even further.

And as you continue to breathe slowly and deeply, feel your body getting heavier, sinking even further into relaxation, taking you away from the stresses and strains of your daily life.

Now imagine that your body is a sponge floating in lovely warm water. Feel yourself lightly floating, the gentle waves perfectly supporting you.

Now imagine that someone is lifting you out of the water, the weight of the water stretching out the sponge, making you taller and taller.

Feel yourself being placed on a flat surface in the full sun, being left there to dry. Think about how you'd be feeling, beautifully warm, your body feeling heavy from the water.

Feel the sun heating you, turning the water into steam. Feel that steam evaporating and leaving your body, making you lighter and lighter, more and more relaxed, completely calm and at peace.

Feeling grief is exhausting. You may have noticed yourself feeling fatigued and stressed recently, which may be a side effect of your grief. Know that it is perfectly normal to feel this way. You may also find yourself feeling angrier than usual or having issues with your memory and focus.

These are all normal and will all go away with time. It's important to practice kindness to yourself as you heal from your loss.

When we break a bone, we recognize that the body will need time to heal and we allow ourselves to rest and recover. The same is true when we suffer a pain. Recognize that your mind needs time to heal and that this process will take as long as it takes. There is no shame in allowing yourself the space you need to heal.

Grief travels through a number of stages that may occur in any order. You may also find that you experience some of them more than once and that's okay. Let your experience be your experience.

You may feel numb, struggling to feel any emotion at all. This is your mind's way of protecting you from the impact of your experience. This numbness gives you time to process what has happened and doesn't mean that you don't care. It just means you're grieving.

You may find yourself feeling angry about what's happened. You might feel angry towards the person or thing you lost, angry at the people you believe are responsible for this loss, angry at God or the universe, angry at the circumstances that led to your loss, angry at people who don't understand what you're going through, even angry at yourself. This anger may be irrational at times and that's okay. It just means you're grieving. As you come to terms with your loss, you will find this anger gradually fades.

You may find yourself questioning why, desperately trying to find an explanation for what happened. You may find yourself trying to bargain with others, with God or the universe, even with yourself, anything to try to undo your loss. Know that there isn't always an explanation for everything, but it's okay to question. It just means you're grieving.

You may find yourself feeling sad and lonely. You may struggle to find the motivation to do anything, even the minimum of self-care. You may find yourself feeling depressed and lacklustre. You may feel confused, suffer from insomnia, find it hard to focus. All these feelings are perfectly normal. They just mean you're grieving. They will go away with time, but you need to allow yourself that time to heal.

Gradually, you will come to a place of acceptance, understanding that life will be different from now on. Different doesn't mean better or worse. It just is. When you are ready, you'll move on. Know that you will get through this.

Let your feelings be your feelings. Let your experience be your experience. It is okay to feel however you feel – anger, sadness, relief, guilt, fear, confusion. These all mean you're grieving and they're all perfectly normal. You are dealing with the situation in your own way and when you come through this, you will be all the stronger for it.

Know that grief can hit you at any time. You will have good days and bad days. Over time, there will be more good than bad, but that doesn't mean you won't ever grieve again. Grief is a journey. Grief is a process. Allow it to be in whatever way feels right for you without judgment.

If you want to shut yourself away and cry, do it. If you want to lose yourself in work, do it. Follow your instincts and grieve in whatever way makes sense to you.

One way that might make it easier for you to deal with your grief is to take time out to sit with the feelings you have. Be with them in the moment, accepting them for what they are and acknowledging that you're grieving.

Take a moment to observe how you're feeling right now and let it be. Let emotions rise and fall without judgment.

Now, in your mind's eye, know that you are in the middle of a peaceful forest. The moon is high in the sky overhead and you hear the sound of owls occasionally hooting in the trees. You are safe and you are secure. There is nothing here that can hurt you.

You are sitting on a log at the edge of a clearing by a campfire. You hear the sound of the fire snapping and crackling, the flames warming you.

In this forest, you have no cares, no worries, no problems. You can give them all to the campfire and let it carry them away.

You realize that there is pen and paper lying on the ground next to you. Pick them up. This is your opportunity to write a letter to someone. It might be someone you've lost or someone responsible for your loss. Whoever you need to talk to right now, write them a letter pouring out your feelings, saying everything you would say if you were able to speak to them right now.

When you have finished writing, fold your letter in half and throw it into the fire. Know that the flames will take your message to the person who needs to hear it, wherever they are.

Now that you've expressed your feelings, you feel so much better. You know that you have permission to feel your grief however you need to.

Inhale deeply and exhale, saying thank you to the forest for allowing yourself to just be.

Inhale deeply again, and as you release this breath, feel yourself becoming more and more awake.

You might like to wriggle your fingers, wriggle your toes.

And when you're ready, open your eyes.

Guided meditation to give you plenty of energy for your day

Meditation is the perfect way to start your morning. I like to meditate before I do anything else. It helps centre my mind and puts me in a good mood that lasts long after my meditation. This meditation will fill you with plenty of energy, making you eager and enthusiastic to get on with your morning.

Make yourself comfortable and close your eyes.

Today is going to be a good day.

Turn your attention to your breath. Inhale deeply and as you exhale, say to yourself, *today is going to be a good day.* You might like to smile as you inhale deeply again, saying to yourself on the exhale, *today is going to be a good day.* Inhale deeply one more time and say out loud, *today is going to be a good day!*

Inhale deeply, sending energy throughout your body and exhaling any tension or fatigue lingering from your sleep.

Now let your breath flow in whatever way feels comfortable, breathing in positivity and breathing out negativity. Know that every breath is energizing you more and more, setting you up to start your day.

Allow that energy to grow, filling you up, invigorating you.

Feel that energy getting bigger and bigger, filling you to overflowing.

Send that energy to your hands and squeeze them tightly into fists. Hold them tighter...tighter...and then release, allowing them to completely relax.

Pull that energy up into your arms. Your arms may feel the urge to lift up, going higher, and higher...and then let them fall, completely relaxed.

As you continue this process, feel yourself filling with excitement and happiness about the day ahead.

Today is going to be a good day.

Send that energy to your feet. Squeeze your feet tightly. Hold them tighter...tighter...and then release, allowing them to completely relax.

Pull that energy up into your legs. They feel the urge to move, to straighten to lift up, or to tense. Let them move higher and higher, then let them completely relax.

Pull that energy up into your head. Scrunch up your face, making it tighter...and tighter...and release, allowing your face to completely relax.

Now send that energy throughout your body. If you want to move, sway, or stretch, just do what your body wants to do.

Tune in to your breath and let your breath connect with your body.

As you breathe in, lift up your right up as high as you can. Lower it as you exhale.

Breathe in and lift your left arm up as high as you can. Lower it as you exhale.

Breathe in and lift both arms up as high as you can. Lower them as you exhale.

Repeat this process for a few cycles.

Breathe in, lift your left arm, breathe out, relax.

Breathe in, lift your right arm, breathe out, relax.

Breathe in, lift both arms, breathe out, relax.

Breathe in, lift your left arm, breathe out, relax.

Breathe in, lift your right arm, breathe out, relax.

Breathe in, lift both arms, breathe out, relax.

Breathe in, lift your left arm, breathe out, relax.

Breathe in, lift your right arm, breathe out, relax.

Breathe in, lift both arms, breathe out, relax.

Now tune into your body, observing how you feel. Notice how you can feel calm and relaxed yet still filled with energy.

Today is going to be a good day.

Now notice a feeling in your stomach, a feeling of excitement, a feeling of positivity, a feeling of potential.

With every breath, send energy down to that feeling, letting it grow bigger…and bigger…

Now see that energy growing without you needing to do anything, filling you with positivity and enthusiasm for the day.

You feel so powerful, so confident, so capable. You are filled with energy, giving you the ability to get everything done you need to.

Today is going to be a good day.

Rub your hands together and feel the energy you create from the friction. As you continue to rub your hands together, it generates plenty of energy for your mind and body, making you feel all refreshed and alert.

Place the palms of your hands over your eyes and feel the reassurance of that warmth.

When you are ready, open your eyes and notice how you feel ready to take on the world.

Today is going to be a good day.

Guided meditation to feel calmer

When we're stressed or under pressure, it can be difficult to stay calm. When we regularly meditate with a focus on calmness, it becomes easier to keep our cool in a crisis.

Go somewhere you won't be disturbed and make yourself comfortable.

Place your left hand on your belly and your right hand on your chest.

Tune into the rhythm of your breath and observe the feeling of your chest rising and falling, your belly rising and falling.

Inhale and feel your chest and belly rise.

Exhale and feel your chest and belly fall.

Now turn your attention to where the breath enters your nose through your nostrils. Feel it flowing in through your nostrils and leaving through your nostrils. Keep your focus on your nostrils and just feel your breath.

Let your attention move away from your nose and just breathe naturally.

Now, on your next inhale, notice your belly rise, the breath coming up to make your ribs expand and your chest lift, coming all the way up to your throat.

As you exhale, watch as your breath leaves the chest, the ribs lower, and your belly pulls in.

Sit with your breath, watching the breath move through the three different areas. As you do, say to yourself *belly, ribs, chest... chest, ribs, belly. Belly, ribs, chest... chest, ribs, belly. Belly, ribs, chest... chest, ribs, belly.*

Let your breathing return to normal.

And on your next inhale, feel the breath flowing easily from your belly and up through your body. Breathe in deeply, hold it for a count of two, then let it go, flowing back down from your chest.

Inhale, hold for a count of two, then exhale.

Inhale, hold for a count of two, then exhale.

Let your breath return to normal.

Notice how you feel so much calmer and connected to yourself.

And when you are ready, open your eyes.

A guided meditation to explore the mind

Your mind is an incredible place. It shapes our perception of the world around us. It can take us to amazing places and motivate us to change our world.

This meditation encourages you to explore the limitless potential of your mind for increased cognitive function.

Go somewhere you won't be disturbed and make yourself comfortable.

Inhale deeply through your nose, hold for a moment, then exhale completely through your mouth.

As you start to connect to your breath, notice if any thoughts are running through your mind. What are they? What are you thinking about in this moment?

Do not follow any particular train of thought, but just be aware that thoughts are there as they come into your mind and then go again.

Watch these thoughts without judgment as you continue to allow your breath to flow.

In a moment, I'm going to describe a number of different scenes. Let your mind picture this scene as soon as you recognize what I'm talking about. Give your mind the freedom to explore without any attachment to a particular place or image. You are a tourist in your own mind, going wherever you will.

Inhale deeply, hold it for a moment, and then release the breath. And when you're ready, let's begin.

In your mind's eye, see:

A lake. A clear, blue lake. A stretch of pebbles next to the lake. A seagull flying over the water. A fish jumping out of the lake. The waters gently lapping the shore. The pebbles. A desert. Tumbleweed in the desert. A brilliant blue sky. A brilliant, blue, cloudless sky. Crickets chirping. A formal garden. A garden with neatly cut grass and trimmed hedges. Dark clouds. A gentle breeze. The tension in the air before the crack of thunder. Dark sky momentarily lit up by lightning. A winding cobblestone path. Fields of lavender. A man walking a dog along the edge of the field. A family having a picnic. The sound of children's laughter. A broad willow tree, the branches hanging over the water. Clear blue sky. Blazing hot sun. Rolling hills and vales. A country mansion. Barns. Cows grazing in the field. The orange of a setting sun. A flock of crows sitting in a tree. The song of a nightingale. The croak of frogs. A rocking chair on a front porch. A jug of ice water. A comfy chair next to an open fire. A shaggy dog lying on the ground. A couple sipping tea. A wall covered in ivy. A thrush cracking open a snail shell. A lounge chair. A mosaic. A bridge over a river. Reflections in the water. An owl hooting. A candle in a window. A candle lighting the dark. A candle flame. A candle flame illuminating the darkness.

Pause for a moment, enjoying the silence.

Inhale slowly and deeply.

Exhale slowly and fully.

And when you are ready, open your eyes.

Guided meditation to relive a happy memory

Sometimes we just want to go back in time to relive a moment that was precious to us. This meditation allows you to go back and experience a time that was very important to you. You can go into this meditation knowing which memory you want to relive, or you can go into it without expectations and simply see what comes up for you.

Go somewhere you won't be interrupted and make yourself comfortable.

Close your eyes and tune into your body. Feel your body relaxing, settling down, becoming calm and peaceful.

Notice your body is starting to feel lighter, lighter, lighter than air. So light you begin to rise up into the air.

Let yourself soar high into the sky. The sun is shining, and the sky is clear with the occasional white cloud. You hear the sound of birds singing and you feel at peace.

Now think back to a favourite memory. Where are you? Know that you can fly there right now, and go there.

Picture the place of that memory in your mind. Think about what it looks like. Think about how it smells. What can you hear? Are you with anyone or are you by yourself? What's happening? How are you feeling? Let yourself be fully in that moment, as if it was happening again right now.

You may like to let yourself smile as you relive this special memory.

When you are ready, rise into the sky again. Look down and see the place where you relived your memory. See how it looks different from a high perspective. You might like to watch yourself relive the memory again, as if it were a movie on a TV screen.

Allow yourself to fly away. You can see a rainbow in the distance, and you fly towards it. Go straight into the rainbow and see yourself surrounded by colours. You can reach out and grab the colours, feel them running through your fingers like water or sand.

As you fly through the rainbow, you see a kite flying nearby. You go after the kite and the kite swoops and darts all over the place. You fly with it, the two of you in a graceful dance high in the sky.

At last, you let the kite go back down to its owner as you continue to fly.

Up ahead, you see a sturdy oak tree. Its branches are thick and strong, and you easily fly down to land safely upon them. You are filled with energy, and you have a wonderful time swinging from branch to branch as you gradually climb back down to the ground.

When you reach the bottom of the tree, sit down on the grass. It is soft and comfortable, and it is easy for you to relax here in the shade of the tree on this beautiful sunny day.

Rest back against the trunk of the tree and just relax. Listen to the birds singing and enjoy the warmth of the sun against your skin, the soft breeze through your hair.

Take your time to enjoy this moment of peace and calm.

When you are ready to return back to reality, start to slowly wriggle your fingers, wriggle your toes. Start to stretch and come back to normality.

When you are ready, open your eyes.

Chapter Summary

- Guided visualizations are one of the most popular ways to meditate.
- You can find guided visualizations online.
- Guided visualizations take you through the process of meditation. All you need to do is relax and follow the instructions.

- Approximately 10% of the population cannot see things in their mind. This is perfectly normal.
- If you cannot visualize, there are other ways to experience these types of meditation. Use your other senses to create the scene in the meditation or simply know that what is being described is around you, rather than pushing yourself to see it.
- You can memorize a visualization script, but it's much easier to meditate if you're listening to it. Either make a recording of yourself speaking or get someone else to read or record the script for you.
- You can adapt the scripts in this chapter to suit your needs.
- After you've finished a guided visualization, remember to journal your experiences. Some guided visualizations are designed to give you messages, information, or guidance on a problem you're currently facing. Writing down these insights can help you get even more out of the meditation when you look back over your notes in the future.

CHAPTER TEN:

FINAL THOUGHTS

"To let go does not mean to get rid of. To let go means
to let be. When we let be with compassion, things come
and things go on their own."

—Jack Kornfield

O nce you start meditating, you've embarked upon a lifelong journey of self-discovery. To quote Betty Rocker, it's a practice, not a perfect. You will have good days and bad days. Even the most experienced meditators will have moments where they struggle to enter a trance state.

You are likely to find that as you progress with your meditation, your tastes change. You may discover that meditation types you struggled with at first become your favourites further down the line. Never be afraid to keep experimenting and exploring. The meditation police will not come to take you away if you stop working with one technique and switch to another!

The benefits of meditation are personal and subtle. It can be difficult to predict what impact it will have on you until you have some experience with meditation. You may find that you don't notice any difference until you stop meditating for a few days. Then you'll see for yourself how meditation has helped you maintain a calm demeanour and respond to challenging situations with thought and compassion. This is why I recommend keeping a meditation journal. In the moment, you may believe you're going to remember breakthroughs that strike you as important, but when you look back over your journal, you'll realize just how much you forget as you travel along your meditation path.

There are as many different ways to meditate as there are meditators. There is no one true way, only what works for you. As long as you are entering into a meditative state (and even that looks different from person to person), it doesn't matter how you get there. This is *your* practice and the only thing that matters is that it works for you.

Remember to be non-judgmental as you develop your meditation practice. Let your experience be your experience without criticism or censure. Accept it for what is – and if you have a session where you find it hard to connect, don't worry about it. There's always next time.

Above all, relax and enjoy yourself. Meditation should be pleasurable and if it's not fun, stop and try another technique. One of the most effective ways to motivate yourself to meditate is to look forward to it because you're going to enjoy yourself so much. If it's a chore, it's just another thing to add to an already overflowing to-do list, which means you won't bother.

When you find a meditation method that works for you, it really can enhance your life in expected and unexpected ways. It can give you a new perspective on events and people, open your eyes to opportunities, and help you change negative ways of thinking and patterns of behaviour. It's scientifically proven to have a positive impact on your physical, mental, and emotional wellbeing and, while it can be used as part of a spiritual practice, it may be just as effective for those with no interest in spiritual matters at all.

It's the ultimate in personal development.

It's my hope that this book will have empowered you to start on your meditation journey. By following the methods outlined on these pages, you have everything you need to begin meditating.

I wish you much joy and inner peace.

Namaste.

THANKS FOR READING

I hope that you enjoyed reading this book and that the lessons and practical exercises have been valuable to you.

If you want to check out more from me, I recommend that you read my books on Stoicism. Stoicism is a powerful philosophy that guides you towards personal improvement and mental growth. They compliment the book you've just read nicely and you'll even find chapters on meditation in them as it is a cornerstone of Stoicism.

I recommend starting with my first book, *Stoicism: How to Use Stoic Philosophy to Find Inner Peace and Happiness*. It's a great place to learn a bit about what Stoicism is and how you can use in your daily life. My second book, *Secrets of the Stoics*, builds on concepts from the first one and reinforces some of the practices you will learn allowing you to become even more immersed in the philosophy.

Once you have learned the concepts from those two books, the next step is to check out my journaling book, *Practicing Stoicism: A Daily Journal with Meditation Practices, Self-Reflections and Ancient Wisdom from Marcus Aurelius.* This book is filled with practical exercises, quotes from ancient philosophers, journaling prompts and self-reflections to teach you how to incorporate Stoicism into your life.

You can view these books here: bouchardpublishing.com/books

Also, be sure to check out my email list, where I am constantly adding tons of value. You will also receive my four-page meditation tracker for free that you can use for reference as you move forward on your meditation journey.

You can sign up here: bouchardpublishing.com/meditation

Lastly, please feel free to join my Facebook group, *Meditation: Find Your Happy Place*, where you can connect with other people interested in meditation. It would be great to see you there.

Kindest regards,
Jason Hemlock

Made in United States
North Haven, CT
12 June 2024

53548506R00078